The Individual
and His Times

D0587451

The Individual
and His Times

a selection of the poetry of

Roy Fuller

Edited by

V.J. Lee

THE ATHLONE PRESS
London

821.91

T 02297

First published 1982 by The Athlone Press Ltd
90–91 Great Russell Street, London WC1B 3PY

© Roy Fuller 1982

*British Library Cataloguing
in Publication Data*

Fuller, Roy
    The individual and his times: a selection
    of the poetry of Roy Fuller.
    I. Title
    821.'912   PR6011.U55

    ISBN 0-485-61008-6

All rights reserved. No part of this publication
may be reproduced, stored in a retrieval system, or
transmitted in any form or by any means, electronic,
mechanical, photocopying or otherwise,
without prior permission in writing from the publisher.

Reprinted 1983

Typset by Inforum Ltd, Portsmouth
Printed in Great Britain by
Nene Litho, Wellingborough, Northants
Bound by Woolnough Bookbinding, Wellingborough, Northants

Contents

Acknowledgments

Acknowledgments are due to André Deutsch Limited for poems in *Collected Poems 1936–1961*, *New Poems*, *Tiny Tears*, *From the Joke Shop* and *Poor Roy*; to London Magazine Editions for poems in *The Reign of Sparrows*.

Introduction

There are times when it seems particularly propitious to offer a selection of a poet's work. Such would seem to be the case with the poetry of Roy Fuller. No selection exists and his *Collected Poems* (André Deutsch, 1962) takes us no further than 1961. Many would argue that much of his finest verse has appeared since then in such volumes as *New Poems* (André Deutsch, 1968) and *The Reign of Sparrows* (London Magazine Editions, 1980).

It is certainly not just a question of availability. Roy Fuller is an extremely versatile poet whose work is marked by a huge variety of theme and tone. This versatility has not always been obvious. One reviewer of *New Poems*, for example, sees it very differently:

> Most of Fuller's verse has in one way or another, been about the role of the poet in a society that is hostile or indifferent to him.

However true that might have been in 1970 when the review was written, it is far too limiting a description of the corpus of Roy Fuller's poetry as it now stands. Here is a poet who is comfortable with the great theme of Time or with the relationship of the poet to his art: he can also make poetry out of a walk through Boots the Chemists ('Strange Meeting', p.3) or the life-cycle of a lungworm ('Autobiography of a Lungworm', p. 84). Although he believes that 'the criterion of success in poetry is brain power', his poems reflect a wide variety of tone. Gentle nostalgia for times past (e.g. 'Aberdeen Revisited', p. 5) rubs shoulders with sheer mirth – but a craftsman's mirth – in the antics of a neighbour's cat ('More about Tompkins', p. 63).

Roy Fuller's poetry is rooted in the Thirties: perhaps he, too, like so many other poets wanted 'to make a new harmony out of strange and apparently ugly material'. Certainly, the Thirties enlarged the area of what was accepted as 'poetic' (see pp. xix–xx).

ix

This broad interpretation of the meaning of poetry, the sheer variety of his interests, and the fact that his poetry spans more than four decades, these help to make him a powerful commentator on the relationship of the individual to our times.

One of the aims of this anthology is to introduce the reader to a representative selection of Roy Fuller's poetry – not representative in the sense that it slavishly includes verse from all his published volumes but in the sense that it covers fairly the poet's range of interests and some of his most accomplished work. To increase the enjoyment of such a selection, some awareness of the social and cultural context is necessary. The poet himself has provided just such an essay which helps to flesh out the context of the poems.

Modern poetry is often attacked because of its alleged incomprehensibility. A problem does arise in Roy Fuller's work because he is, at times, a poet of implicit meaning. The qualification is necessary, because a poem such as 'Happiness' (p. 70) or 'End of the Cheap Food Era' (p. 71) needs no comment. In addition, there is a riddling or enigmatic aspect about some of his poetry which is part of the poetic technique and which has a long and respectable tradition in English, dating back to the Anglo-Saxon period. That said, there are occasions when the meaning of a word, line or poem can only be reclaimed by an allusion which, itself, is not explained in the poem. For example, the meaning of the word 'square' in the following line is difficult to fathom without some knowledge of the scientific background (see note):

> Learning how square waves were to guard old England.
> ('Aberdeen Revisited', l.6)

Or again taking extreme examples, 'Florestan to Leonora' (p. 33) or 'Oxford Album' (p. 71) only make fullest sense with some knowledge of Beethoven's *Fidelio* and the Stuttgart Opera Company's performance of it, or of Oxford and Roy Fuller's holding of the Professorship of Poetry there. It is with this type of allusion, which affects meaning, that the Notes attempt to be of help. In other words, while emphasizing the primacy of the poetry, this text can be most gainfully used if all three parts are used in conjunction: poems, introductory essay and notes.

The text itself is divided into six sections, each section representing what the editor has judged to be a major interest of the poet.

The sections are not intended as watertight groupings. A sound case could be made for including 'The Lawn, Spring and Summer' (p. 6) under *Nature*, for instance – but they are intended as coherent groupings around the poet's thematic interests.

The sections are grouped internally in what has been deemed to be the most appropriate way to draw a new reader into Roy Fuller's treatment of that particular theme. (There is no attempt at a strict chronology, but, it is hoped, a merely perverse arrangement has been avoided.) The war poems (Section Four), for example, follow a gentle chronology in terms of the events they describe, but not in terms of when they were written. The first four poems in that section were written during the Second World War, but were not published in their present form until 1974, and then only in limited numbers by a private press. 'Memories of War' (p. 54), although published after 'Confrontation off Korea, 1968' (p. 54), precedes it in this edition, as it seems to the editor a fitting conclusion to the poems of the Second World War.

The Poet of Everyday Life (Section Five) is probably the section where the arrangement is most *ad hoc*. The three 'family' poems start the section, followed by the five 'animal' poems. Such is the range of Roy Fuller's subjects here that it is impossible to give a reasonably representative sample and pretend there is one compelling order in which they should be read. By the end of the section, 'Books and Discs', 'The Night Sky in August 1980' and 'Abbas' are largely in that position on chronological grounds, as recent poems, although it was considered a strong ending to finish the section with the series of quatrains, 'Abbas'. These last three poems are part of a group of nine poems included in this selection which have not been published previously, other than in journals or private printings.

When presenting a selection of the verse of a living poet, the best source of information can be the poet himself. Roy Fuller has been a constant source of assistance in this respect, unfailing in his courtesy and kindness.

Victor Lee

15 December 1981

xi

The Individual and His Times

Schooldays and after

I suppose I ought to start with my schooldays, spent mostly at private schools far less well equipped than schools of any kind today. In the very early Nineteen-twenties, when I was about ten years old, a schoolmistress asked the class to copy into notebooks lines of poetry that appealed to them. I was alarmed. There were no books of verse at home, and at school the only poetry I had access to was Canto 1 of Sir Walter Scott's *Lay of the Last Minstrel*, which we were 'doing' in class. I copied into my notebook a sententious verse that I recalled my grandmother had written in my autograph album, and the following line from *The Lay of the Last Minstrel*: 'O swiftly can speed my dapple-grey steed'. Whether I ever added to this meagre anthology I do not recall.

I had read in the notes or (less likely) the teacher had expounded, that the movement of Scott's line imitated, in its speed and undulations, the movement of the horse. This aptness greatly appealed to me, and rightly so, for its power to embody such gimmicks is an indication of poetry, differentiating it from prose.

Later in my schooldays, though short-story writing was what I longed to succeed at, I came to write a poem or two myself, output increasing after I left school at sixteen to become a solicitor's articled clerk – a 'trainee solicitor' as it is genteely termed today. At the age of four or five I had become passionately devoted to reading, still am. Myself providing reading matter seemed at first a way to fame along an agreeable road. I hoped it might in the end be a full-time occupation, as it was for the literary giants of my boyhood, G.B. Shaw, H.G. Wells, Arnold Bennett. In the result it remained for by far the greater part of my adult life a 'spare-time' occupation. I always realised, of course, that my verse would never earn me a living, but it also turned out that my novels were too highbrow, or maybe just not good enough, to be popular.

The Depression and after

It also turned out that my boyhood ended at the start of a world upheaval, which led to an upheaval in English writing, particularly the writing of poetry. The economic 'blizzard' (as it was called) of 1929 and ensuing years produced not only mass unemployment but also the rise of Hitler, the spread of the barbarous and repressive phenomenon of fascism, the threat and finally the virtual certainty of a second world war. It cannot be said that before 1929 one lived in a just, prosperous and ordered England: I had arrived at socialistic beliefs under my own steam at school, conscious of the injustices and illogicalities in the distribution of money and privileges in society. But that had not affected the kind of poetry I wrote, which I suppose aimed at depicting, embodying, 'beauty'. I put the word in inverted commas not to denigrate it (for undoubtedly concepts of the beautiful must enter into all creative activity) but to indicate the vagueness of my endeavour. All my poems of those days are fortunately lost, but some dealt with the beauty of the beloved, fewer with that of nature, and I guess most of them would try to use 'beautiful' words in a 'beautiful' way.

By 1932 my socialism had become 'scientific socialism', that is Marxism. I believed that the wrongs in society could be righted only through social revolution; that the threat of war could be removed only by the victory of the international working-class; and that effective opposition to the Nazi and other fascist movements would only effectively come from radical left-wing parties, or under their leadership. By that date the poets W.H. Auden, Stephen Spender and C. Day Lewis had published their early books, all containing verse concerned with social issues and political beliefs. One began to feel oneself a part of a new movement in literature, sharing a feeling echoed in the names of periodicals and anthologies of the time – *New Signatures, New Writing, New Country, New Verse*.

'Bliss was it in that dawn to be alive, /But to be young was very heaven' – did one feel in those very early years of the Nineteen-thirties as Wordsworth did about the French Revolution? Not at all. Almost from the start there were difficulties and unhappiness for the contemplative intellectual, which, after all, is what a poet is. In my own case I can deal quite simply with what, for others, became an issue of great moment and much spilt ink. The belief in Marxism, with the usual corollary belief in the virtue of the existence and even all the actions of the Soviet Union, seemed to some a matter of faith. On losing that faith they felt deeply guilty at ever having held it, particularly, perhaps, if they moved instead into religious beliefs. After the war, a collection of essays about this loss of faith in communism was indeed given the title *The God That Failed*. My own scepticism was slow-developing, not accompanied by any dramatic withdrawal from party politics, not turning into religiosity. I grew to be ambivalent about the goodness of mankind in the mass, and about State ownership and other things underlying socialism. I would guess that my attitude at the time of the death of Stalin is quite well shown by 'Death of a Dictator': maybe I should by then have been more uncomplicatedly anti-Stalinist, but the sonnet hints at the far from straightforward feelings of the past.

A more lasting source of unease was the developing sense that, almost by definition, the 'contemplative intellectual' was temperamentally and otherwise unfitted for political life and action. This may seem more trivial than the question of belief, and so indeed it is. Yet is exercised my mind both before and after the war, exercises it still to some extent, for the evils of the age go on presenting themselves as conquerable, if at all, only by active steps to be taken by each individual – or, at any rate, as so pervasive and fundamental as to make taking no steps a matter of self-reproach. In my early days, when the new-found dogmas of scientific socialism seemed a complete answer to the world's ills, I despised any viewpoint short of utter Marxist belief, and committed political action on behalf of the working-class. Before the war, Stephen Spender (whose poetry I much admired) advanced the idea that a poet might usefully and more honestly write from a standpoint of weakness – write out of his doubts about dogma, his flinching from action, his scruples about ruthlessness – but in those days I would have called this bourgeois softness, as would many young dogmatists still. Yet it may be said that in the end I wrote almost all my poetry from that standpoint or a similar one.

There are none of those 'dogmatic' poems in this book. In fact, I excluded them, as too unsatisfactory, from my first collection of verse, *Poems*, which came out in 1939. There is nothing in this book from *Poems* either, no great loss. If looked at, *Poems* would show the problems of the world and the life of the poet pretty well hidden behind masks of poetic styles and poetic forms. The book is a suitable reminder to us to bear in mind, when talking about the subject, that every poet cuts into English literature, as it were, at a certain point in the game, when all sorts of what may be called purely literary preoccupations exist. How can I get away from the heroic couplet? some young poet might have asked himself in the early eighteenth century. In the early twentieth century plenty of poets decided to get away from the iambic pentameter. There is much – most! – to poetry that is not ideology. Similarly it should be remembered that the 'I' of a poem is not necessarily the poet himself, even when it seems to be. The poet would be an intolerable egotist if he did not feel that as a poet he wore a mask that more often than not resembles other men. I think that is why in his verse he can be free with the details of his personal life – give himself away as a lesson, not a confession.

War

The earliest poems in this selection are from the war years. Being called up into the Royal Navy in 1941 made irrelevant for the time being the division between the withdrawn poet and the wicked world, the privileged solicitor and the under-privileged working-man. It came to me quite soon that the poems I hoped to write about being in the armed forces should be relatively simple. Like Wilfred Owen in the First World War, I did not want, as he said, 'to write anything to which a soldier would say No Compris.' 'Waiting To Be Drafted' is a good example – even the form is simple, just the short last lines of the stanzas with the same rhyme. 'YMCA Writing Room' is simple, too, especially if compared with many things in *Poems*, though Owen's soldier might have to ponder more. For instance, the 'blues and reds' of the map are 'dangerous' because blue indicates sea, dangerous in wartime, and red the

British Empire (it existed then), empire being a phenomenon a socialist would consider as making for war.

I had a lucky war, and in 1946 returned to my pre-call-up position as a solicitor with a large building society, having published two collections of poetry during the war.

The Anti-Hero

I will now enlarge on what I said earlier about the notion of writing poetry frankly from a position of weakness. I hope it would be too limiting to say that all my poetry since the war shows up the writer as an 'ineffectual angel' (Matthew Arnold's phrase for Shelley), because it does take account of the ironies of the position, and does not pretend to have engagements with the word that its author lacks. 'The Ides of March' perhaps puts the business in its starkest terms. Brutus, not quite the historical or Shakespearian Brutus, is presented as a previously uncommitted man about to throw in his lot with a terrorist faction. Contrary to what might be imagined, using a literary-historical character rather than making the 'I' of the poem more personal, enables the subject to be treated with a good deal of enriching freedom. For instance, the poem refers to the legend that Brutus was Caesar's natural son, and so is brought in obliquely the Freudian idea of the Oedipus Complex, the repressed wish of a son to kill his rival the father.

At this time, the mid-Fifties, the personification so appealed to me that I called the collection in which 'the Ides of March' appeared *Brutus's Orchard*. The title was meant to indicate that in a sense all the poems were set in a place where the love for wife and children, and the wish to create, were threatened by tyrants, injustice – and the urgings of conspirators. In such a place one could not remain for ever, or without guilt. But another poem of the same period, 'Florestan to Leonora', shows how far I had come from the strict ideology of the early Thirties. Florestan is daunted at the idea of being freed into a just and happy world, having grown used to, been stimulated by, a world of dictatorial oppression, complicated art, and unjust imprisonment. The poem was prompted by my seeing a production of Beethoven's *Fidelio* by the Stuttgart Opera Company, where the whole action was designed to take place behind enormous prison bars, under a regime suggestive of Nazism, which had then only fairly recently been overthrown. I had also in mind my puzzlement, on a committee to further Anglo-Soviet cultural relations just after the war, at the sparseness of Soviet novels except those displaying a naive black and white morality, and shallowness of characterization.

It would be foolish to wish poetry to be simple all the time. The poems here will show (as do those of so many modern writers) the heritage of art and science that has come down to us, and the complications of human beings, which psychoanalysis, as well as ordinary observation, reveals. As readers will find, perhaps to their vexation, I feel observations about culture have just as much a place in poetry as observations about nature: for instance, the citing of Kierkegaard and Sorel in 'In his Sixty-Fifth Year' being as legitimate as the comparison of twigs to mandarins' long fingernails in 'Pictures of Winter' (the latter possibly a hangover from my boyhood reading of the Dr Fu Manchu stories).

The admission by the poet, or the 'I' of a poem, of doubts and ambivalences and so forth, is not always carried on in such solemn terms as those of Beethoven's opera or Shakespeare's Roman tragedy. The ironies of human existence extend to politics and sociology, nominally serious matters. In 'Translation', the anti-radical viewpoint is exaggerated so as to ram the points home and provide amusement – though it may be hazarded that the author in real life sometimes had such thoughts himself. Again, in 'Chinoiserie', the opposition between the characters of poet and man of business existing in the same human envelope, is put in a way that will divert, perhaps slightly shock, the reader: the actual possessor of such characters may be imagined to regard and combine them in a deeper and more subtle way.

Thinking about the poet's 'masks', which may be found throughout this book (even the 'elderly man' of later poems cannot be guaranteed to be the poet himself, though in this case I feel there is an obligation on the poet not to over-act!), the extreme case may be thought to be the piece where the 'I' is a parasite of the pig ('Autobiography of a Lungworm').

The parallels between the decline of the Roman Empire and of institutions (including the British Empire) in the modern age, have encouraged me to don antique masks. This is especially true of 'On the Mountain', where the Emperor Constantine's Rome has a distinctly up-to-date look, and the analogy between primitive Christianity and modern communism is exploited.

Cold War

Soon after the war, the opposition between Russia and the West brought the threat of a new war, with a horrifying ingredient added – the atom bomb, which had already been senselessly dropped. As it turned out, the peace was prolonged, but I have expressed the fear of nuclear conflict in many post-war poems, perhaps too many, for the horror of Hiroshima and Nagasaki haunts me, and so I am apt to bring the business into poems which strictly do not demand it. It may be thought the last one and a half lines of 'An English Summer' is such a case. Many of the sensations of living in these times are put in concentrated form in the separate quatrains of 'Confrontation Off Korea, 1968', which was an actual historic incident that for some days seemed likely to bring about open hostilities between East and West.

Ordinary Life

The prolonged peace, and my own living into old age and going on writing, meant that my poetry has reflected a good deal of what may be called ordinary life. Readers stipulating for romanticism or excitement may object that there was no obligation on me either to continue versifying or to versify diurnal existence. I suppose I myself, at the very start of trying to write poetry, would have been incredulous had I been told that one day I would compose a poem about walking through Boots the Chemists (see 'Strange Meeting'). But one of the effects of the 'new' poetry of the early Thirties was to enlarge the area of the 'poetic': indeed, the rule became that there was nothing that was not poetic. As Auden put it in his introduction to a schools' anthology of 1935 (*The Poet's Tongue*) poetry is 'memorable speech':

About what? Birth, death, the Beatific Vision, the abysses of hatred and fear, the awards and miseries of desire, the unjust

xix

walking the earth and the just scratching miserably for food like hens, triumphs, earthquakes, deserts of boredom and featureless anxiety, the Golden Age promised or irrevocably past, the gratifications and terrors of childhood, the impact of nature on the adolescent, the despairs and wisdoms of the mature, the sacrificial victim, the descent into Hell, the devouring and the benign mother? Yes, all of these, but not these only. Everything that we remember no matter how trivial: the mark on the wall, the joke at luncheon, word games, these, like the dance of a stoat or the raven's gamble, are equally the subject of poetry.

We shall do poetry a great disservice if we confine it only to the major experiences of life . . .

This view of Auden's is perhaps a commonplace today. Or at any rate, lip service is paid to it, though I wonder whether people still don't feel deep down that poets should put on special singing robes, and the product itself have a special seriousness of content and tone. Edith Sitwell was always scathing about my having written a poem concerning a lungworm; the fact that she had misread it as being a lugworm, rather an inferior article, being not much to the point.

One effect of the coming of Auden, augmenting the coming of T.S. Eliot twenty years earlier, was to remove from poetry the obligation to be 'beautiful', an obligation perhaps specifically a hangover from the Eighteen-nineties. I mean really, that 'beauty' was no longer in the forefront of the poet's mind; his aim in writing poetry something other.

> Went to the Mini-Town Hall
> (So-called) to claim my free
> Pass for the off-peak bus.

At the start of my poem 'On His Sixty-Fifth Birthday', the low tone, the everyday detail, unselfconsciously appear. Nevertheless, poetry is poetry and not prose, a distinction in these times often overlooked. It is interesting, certainly to the poet, what notions are poetic and what – I will not say 'prosaic', for that begs the question – are better cast in prose. The question quite often comes up, and I give an example I see at this moment on my desk in the form of a scribbled note. After the death a decade ago of an old friend, a pianist, I was given by his widow the tapes he had recorded from the radio and the discs over the years. Running one of them the other day, I came across a stretch previously unheard, what must have been the youthful, newly-exiled Vladimir Ashkenazy playing (marvellously) Debussy's 'Voyage à Cythère', a favourite of mine. At once several emotions arose. But their demand for expression in a poem seems hardly likely to be fulfilled because of the detail that would be required to put the reader in possession of the 'plot' of the poem before the poignancies and ironies of the situation could be communicated. *Per contra*, the first line of the first of the 'Quatrains of an Elderly Man' immediately sets the scene, and enables the 'story' of the brief poem to be directly told.

Poetry is, on the whole, a succinct art; accordingly the reader must let it expand in his understanding. Perhaps it is worth saying at this point that I doubt if there is anything arbitrary in the poems that follow. I hope everything may in the end be seen to hold meaning, possibly more than one. A simple example, maybe too obvious, is 'chemical/Warfare against our little green invaders', in 'Hedge-Sparrows and House-Sparrows', where the terms used for a gardener's tactics against greenfly remind the reader of the science-fiction cliché of little green men from outer space. One wants – of course – such *double entendres* to be perceived, but some academics have encouraged readers to go too far, trying to tease out meanings in poetry that the poet never intended. The rule for the reader should be that he try to make sure he understands the *means* of a poem. Though the poet's intention may be not to write beautifully but (say) to poke fun at a world where a Third War is 'on' almost immediately after a Second, the means used are poetic means. Even in the lungworm poem there are alliterative and onomatopoeic phrases the poet was rather pleased to bring forth, such as 'Far from the scarlet and sustaining lung'. Apropos of the 'poetic', I have often felt science to be somehow intrinsically poetic, no doubt because of its close connection with the meticulous observation of reality. Hence part of the attraction of the lungworm's life cycle.

I count myself lucky that as a very young poet I fell under the spell of Auden mainly because he showed so clearly how the traditional forms of poetry could continue to be used. In the Nineteen-twenties free verse was extremely fashionable, and Auden's using in his early book, the 1930 *Poems*, a metre like that of Tennyson's 'Locksley Hall' came as a shock – and a stimulus:

> Get there if you can and see the land you once were proud to
> own
> Though the roads have almost vanished and the expresses
> never run:
> Smokeless chimneys, damaged bridges, rotting wharves and
> choked canals,
> Tramlines buckled, smashed trucks lying on their side across
> the rails . . .

Who would have imagined England's industrial depression of the time expressed in such couplets, in theory so artificial? Had it not been for Auden surely I would never, thirty-five years later, have cast my observations and emotions at T.S. Eliot's memorial service in the metre of Tennyson's 'To Virgil', couplets with even longer lines.

The burden laid on those who work in traditional forms is to avoid being in the wrong sense 'poetic'. What is written should still be 'speech', however elaborate the form, though it would be too puritanical to think that that always excluded the sonorous:

> The coloured scutcheons of the founding earls
> Dim libraries of brown or golden hair.
> The dreams of dons are dwarfs and little girls.
>
> ('Oxford Album')

I should add that I have used free verse, and also syllabic metres – in the latter case merely counting the syllables in a line, regardless of stress. Thus 'Creeper' consists of lines each nine syllables long, if my arithmetic was correct, the general effect being to make the poem sound in paragraphs rather than lines. I would now make my line-endings more emphatic than they are in this and other syllabic poems – probably not allowing the termination 'the', as in line four of the first stanza. But these scruples are probably more bother-some to the poet than to the reader.

The Double (or Treble) Life

After the war, as I have said, I returned to my job as solicitor to a building society. I was with the Woolwich, as a matter of fact. In 1958, in my mid-forties, I started to assume greater and wider legal responsibilities. I had always imagined fading away, like an old soldier, from the world of affairs when I was better known as a writer and family responsibilities had lessened. In the event the position was reversed. Though I wrote novels regularly, and did a fair amount of literary journalism, I could not at any time have easily existed as a whole-time author. But getting more interested and involved in the law was a turn I had not bargained for. It must be admitted that moonlighting as a writer, though I was well accustomed to it, was not ideal; though I believe that no writer's material life, however it may be contrived, in any way approaches the ideal.

When I was asked to stand for the Oxford Professorship in 1968 I was prepared to make it a third strand in my life (the duties are not onerous), but soon after I was elected I was appointed to the Board of Directors of my building society, not a full-time job, and retired as its solicitor and as legal advisor to the Building Societies Associa-tion, which I had also been. I was fifty-seven, and so had spent the bulk of my working life in a dual role. Hardly had I cleared the decks for more freedom to write, when I consented to be appointed to the BBC's Board of Governors, on which I served for nearly eight years. So I have been fated never really to sever my links with 'ordinary' life, if that is to be thought of as somehow distinct from the life of a poet.

I give these personal details not least to emphasize the overlap-ping of 'ordinary' life and 'poetic' life. As to the latter, one is not blessed a hundred per cent of one's time with the power to make poetry, which activity is not merely a sensitivity to impressions and words but also – perhaps especially – a conviction that one is in the groove to arrange impressions and words rhythmically, a matter already touched on or implied. 'Spiders in wellington boots in garden sheds': one may note such a thing, but can the observation and what may follow from it logically or illogically, be cast into rhythmical form? – the dapple-grey steed business in rather trickier term. So a non-poetic life may come in useful.

Poetry's Duties

I do not worry today about my (and other 'highbrow') poetry being cut off from a mass readership, as I used to worry at the start of the Thirties, thinking there was something limiting in intellectualism, and that people would be more interested if the poet wrote of their political aspirations and social deprivations; feeling, too, that the 'people' had a poetic tradition, which the highbrow or intellectual poet should come out to meet half way. I see now what may be thought painfully obvious, that in any society the poet needs independence of thought and expression, is likely to be deficient as a man of action, and, more often than not, too much of a leg-puller to appeal to such as politicians. While I would not go as far as Auden, who came in the end to say that poetry had absolutely no effect in directing human life, certainly it operates far differently from propaganda. My poems may keep homing in on the menace of nuclear war, but they can do nothing to divert it: however, they may encourage that 'species absurd – the timid' (see 'Confrontation Off Korea, 1968').

In the course of writing this, I came across, in the *Times Literary Supplement*, a phrase by the historian Peter Green, chilling but I believe accurate, describing the present time as 'an era of bankrupt morality and collapsing social values'. Besides poetry's duty not to be bad poetry, I still think it should try, even in vain, to save morality and uphold social values.

Roy Fuller

One

The Passage of Time

Diary Entries

'I'll burn it off now if you like,' said my GP,
Apropos of the papilloma on my thigh,
Bothersome of late. Would that all worries
Disappeared in a whiff of over-done pork!

*

5 An aircraft's linear trail on the evening sky
From apple bough to pink hibiscus – first
Speculative but bold foundation of a web
That fades as the predator sees no hope of victims.

*

A negative report on the specimen
10 Of urine. So am I after all to live
Into the epoch of apocalyptic beasts
And utterly depersonalized demise?

*

Giving away old suits – preparation
For a journey. The letting-out of waistbands –
15 Dicing with the proximity
Of terminal emaciation.

*

Even peeing in the garden, giving moisture
To a shaded plant, organic nurture

1

To legginess, mad midges presaging heat,
20 Also brings gloomy thoughts of malignant strictures.

*

Deep in the medicine-chest are remedies
For ills it seems I no longer suffer from.
What forgotten wounds have made me the man I am?
Where's the historical record of my health?

*

25 Through numbness the arm behind feels amputated;
The arm in front is hovering in the air.
Can it be at the age of fifty-nine
I haven't learnt how to dispose my limbs for sleep?

*

A good thing on waking to drink cold water
30 Through the nose (I read in some Yogi handbook).
A good thing also to stop writing verses
About one's ailments and daydreams of romance.

*

Old theatre programme: against the Second Lord,
Great heroes' name. A file of ancient verse
35 Above the signature, evidently spurious,
Of a quite accomplished reactionary hermit.

*

Dear life, I struggle awake to greet you again –
Fetching the honeyed hot milk, finding my father's
Cigarette-case among the debris of yesterday's pockets,
40 Realising that after all it's not you that frightens us.

Strange Meeting

In Boots the Chemists an oldish fellow bars my way –
An eye to eye encounter as I try to pass
Into another part of the emporium.

He wears a sober navy overcoat. His hair's
5   Indubitably salt and pepper. His regard
Is one of semi-recognition, tinged with alarm.

As may already have been guessed, I've misconceived
A mirrored wall as a communicating door.
I turn with a muttered oath: the old boy disappears.

10   The young boy still continues on his foolish course.

Death of a Dictator

The children years ago made their escape
Out of the father's tense, oppressive field:
His moral scheme was of too strict a shape
To hold the freedom that their growth revealed.

5   Now he lies bound and senseless up the stair,
Drowned by the failing channels of his flesh,
They momentarily return and wear
The old familiar pressure of the mesh.

They wait among the ugly furniture,
10   Rich with the poignant memories of their youth:
Once more they feel that agonising blur –
The hopeless falsehood merging into truth.

And still perceive a sprig of what their hate
Grew up with and then choked – but all too late.

At T. S. Eliot's Memorial Service

A man comes on the stage clad in a robe different from all others,
with lute in hand on which he plays, and thus chants the Great
Mysteries, not knowing what he says.

JESSIE L. WESTON: *From Ritual to Romance*

Arches cut across each other, open out within each other, till
Winter sky the shade of old men's hair appears beyond the
final sill.

Rectangles of iron-tubing for the pensile lamps draw down
the eye
To the choir-stalls' vandyke timber and their submarine
upholstery.

5 Here the lights themselves seem gloomy: golden stalks with
single crimson flowers.
Distant pallid busts the monuments of poets longer dead
than ours.

In the drama set to show the spirit's primacy and endlessness
Piping choir-boys pustular remind one of its transitory
dress.

Revolutionary writer of my youth, how far must it have
been
10 From imagination so to see you to the brink of the unseen;

And in your relating of the myth to find at last that it was
thus
Fell the strange and frightening adventure in the Chapel
Perilous –

Which is fraught, we're made to understand, with danger
indefinable:

4

Details vary; sometimes on the altar there is laid a lifeless
    shell . . .

15 Suddenly I notice that the arms that isolate me in my place
Are the backward-spreading wings of angels each with
    polished plump-cheeked face.

Simple craftsman's image, words and chords by more
    sophisticated pens,
Celebrate the sad illusion that the mortal nerves and brain
    make sense.

Tributory bowler on its not entirely unaccustomed head,
20 Leaving through the great West Door, bells muffled for the
    now-accepted dead.

All is changed until I see that it's Victoria Street and not the
    Square
Lies before me, purgatory-crowded, hideous in the sharpen-
    ing air –

Half expecting one to hail me, marks of mould upon him,
    grave of tone:
'Wounded still the Ruler, waterless the land, omnipotent the
    bone'.

Aberdeen Revisited

The gulls laugh madly in the rainy dawn.
Smell of stale fish pervades the railway station –
Indeed, the quays and cobbles and my heart.

Thirty and three years past I sojourned here –
5 Staggeringly lucky hide-out from the War –
Learning how square waves were to guard old England.

I turn left, have to ask my way: it seems
My *alma mater's* to the theatre's left.
My tear-filled eyes gaze down a viaduct.

10 How sad it is about a life that's gone –
Whether about its passing or its mode
Or abdicated ecstasies, who knows?

Yes, I was young and happy here, though bothered
By fate in ways that now seem ludicrous,
15 And would have guiltily felt blessed to think

More than three decades on I should be searching
For where the Andrew let me live in digs,
And sending postcards to my grand-daughters.

Orderly streets of brownish, greyish stone!
20 Two drunks – flushed, agitated – stagger past: they were
A little boy and girl in those far days –

Days of impossibly idyllic health;
Days when bad states were doomed, when only guns
Could kill; days that will never come again.

The Lawn, Spring and Summer

Presumably ejected by the mother,
Three ochre scraps of skin, just avian:
Aborted result of the long and hungry sitting,
Brief tenants of a nest miraculous
5 As landscapes drawn with toes, the wasted weeks
Of a season crucial and counted out in weeks.
I salute your ruthless clearing of the decks,
Blackbird, for further action. And, dismayed,
Am seized again with Nature's heroic nature,
10 So different from my own; what's more, see called
In question culture's terminology.

6

'Nature' – quite ludicrous to subsume in that
The gods' and scavengers' approach to death,
The brusquest concentration of the art
15 Of the possible – the only art that bridges
Dying and dead societies, those species
Extinct and those that scheme against extinction,
The temperate mantle from its boiling end.

But if confronted by a similar call
20 To start once more, then wouldn't one contrive
To love afresh survival's ancient means,
And court on the very mattress of the dead?
What else but summoning of feeble power
Distinguishes the organic from the rest?

25 And isn't one precisely so confronted
This Spring and Summer of one's Autumn life?
The window shut against the noise of brakes,
Ascending gears, and aircraft, nonetheless
Bad dreams remain – made by inferior fears,
30 The penalty of being here at all.
This is our nature, only overcome
By trying to disremember what we love,
The individual life included, grass
Littered with history's debris; and the will
35 Loud in rosetted branches, master of air,
Preparing generations for the wars
And thwarted happiness. Not bad, old tree-rat,
I think, encountering in the hard, late lawn
A green and reasonably buried walnut.
40 Anticipate the ice-age as you can,
Anticipate the burning should it come,
Live with your death, your species' death – with craft,
That on this globe, and those unknown and past,
The gases and the carbon spirals clasp
45 A spirit fearful but immortal somewhere.

Thirty Years On

I take from the shelves a book of '42
And blow the dust out of the upper edge
And open at the flyleaf quite by chance

And see my mother's love and Christmas wish
5   In her distinctive hand, addressed to me.
Blindingly, more than half my life comes back.

Obviously she was prompted in the choice –
The book being Francis Scarfe's on '30s poets!
Where was I then? In darkest Africa?

10   Her writing's vivid still because the pen
Was held between her first and second fingers.
She could be still alive, at 84.

The reason for my getting down the book
Is to see what it says of Kenneth Allott,
15   Just dead, born in my year of 1912.

My mother was no older when she died
Than he was, or I am. Good God, the years
Spell irony however they're cast up!

How tickled she'd have been at honours since
20   Acquired – the trivia of longevity
Made worthwhile for her sake.

Thinking of Allott, he by '42
Had uttered what the grudging genius
Of verse was to permit;

25   Though there is consolation for all those
Who loved him – as Sibelius said: 'Preserve
The themes of your youth: the best you will invent.'

I was too immature to write or care
Effectively by 1942:
30   The speech choked back, frustrated audience gone.

Faint memory of Christmas of that year:
A Whitmanesque night-passage through the camp;
Ratings with branches, bottles; all dead drunk.

It's certain that I never sent my thanks
35   So as to touch my mother's worried heart;
And now, in Allott's words, 'Too late. Too late.'

My father, before his youthful death, would find
Because of fingers-slotted pen, his bride
Of twenty-one a fascinating scribe.

40   Strangely, the feeling is alive today;
And his undoubted thankfulness for life,
And creativity.

from
In His Sixty-fifth Year

The October of his Sixty-fifth Year

With beak about as long and hinged as chopsticks,
The starling stabbing among the chocolate whorls
Is speckled like a specimen of quartz,
Except the slanted settings for the eyes
5   Which are as dark as those of belly-dancers.

Strange that obsessive observation seems
To be an overture to verse – as strange
As wriggling food preceding avian art.

Should old age act as though its missing teeth
10   And fading sight were mere stage properties
Irrelevant to its response to life –

9

Which ought to be as though demise were still
As lightly contemplated as in youth?

Ideal arrangement; rarely met, however –
15   Like that prescription of the Danish sage:
'It's a good thing for monarchs to be ugly.'

Bird-brains somewhat exaggeratedly
Counter the seasons' revolutions: man's
Presumably perturb them not at all.

20   Not for them huge errors of intelligence
Like Sorel's, who before the First World War
Tried to enoble violence, which he thought
Was on the downgrade – to the detriment
Of efficacious social struggle – though
25   In Fact a Time of Troubles loomed. Still here!

Maniacs salute annihilating missiles,
And English-beetle nourished nightingales
Winter among the zebras of Zaire.

Singing, 1977

For most of my life, no need to wear specs.
30   Now I look over them at meetings
With the aplomb of a rotten actor,
Push them around my bumf when spouting,
Needlessly checking the earpieces' hinges.
Of all my portraits I say: poor likeness.
35   'Colonel (Retired)' or 'Disgusted' stares out,
Doomed to expire of apoplexy;
Whitening moustache, jaw-line sagging.
Like a woman, I think: I've lost my looks.
Reactionary views, advanced mostly
40   To raise a laugh – taken as gospel!

I've bought these discs of piano music
By Granados – largely unexplored;
And if asked who I'd take to a desert island,

Him or who'd be just as novel, Schoenberg,
45 Who doubts an elderly buffer would choose
The melodious Debussyan Spaniard?

As a matter of fact I'd not mind taking
The words and music of Johnny Mercer,
Even discounting what really biffs me –
50 That after the euphemistic 'long illness'
He died in a year of his seventh decade
(Strange years, and each year seeming more strange),
The departed gold summer of '76.
Only the weather will return in the vintage,
55 Perhaps a corked bottle or two recalling
How bitter some days were to swallow,
Prompting thanks for more commonplace years.

Mercer's pushing the case, of course;
As we do in Cheltenham or Tunbridge Wells.
60 My life's been a story of ignorance.
I never even used to know
How spiders adhered to walls in winter
(Like blots that need blowing up to be decoded),
Challenging man to accept hibernation;
65 That wind keeps old folk, like babies, wakeful.
No record made: passion undeclared.

At the junketings for my son's sixty-fifth
I'll be pinching his thunder by nearing
My ninetieth. Not that he'll mind.
70 Jerome Kern's 'They'll never believe me'
(Pre-dating the torpedoing of Granados!)
And that mysterious Mercer line,
As though from an Edwardian operetta:
'There's a dance pavilion in the rain' –
75 Things I so often sing, by then
Mad time will have made even quainter.

But could I possibly still own a voice?
Curious enough at sixty-five –
A blessing, too; that sons may note at forty –
80 Even though one messes about perversely,
Trying, say, four-beat unrhymed lines
Which no decent poet, except Arthur Waley,
Has ever managed to get off the ground.

And why so ego-centred the content?
85 Emblematic, I try to persuade myself,
Of the entire human condition –
Composers who die in usual pain,
Who drown, meaning to rescue their wives,
Regular soldiers, rain-moulded dancers,
90 Work of joy and disappointment,
Life of creativeness and bereavement . . .
Peering at some enigmatic blot,
Groping for my glasses in the night-time.

On his Sixty-fifth Birthday

Went to the Mini-Town Hall
(So-called) to claim my free
Pass for the off-peak bus.
No one expressed surprise
5 That I was sixty-five –
Stunned at my sprightly gait
And thick if frosted hair.
The ladies around were concerned
With reduced-price Ovaltine
10 And other baksheesh of the State,
Befitting unamorous age.

The tawdry building was set
In bogland off the A2:

12

Blown paper white as the gulls
15 On the stud-dented fields of play
Deserted now in the sun –
Shot end of a winter day
By home-wending girls and boys.
O feet-distorting shoes,
20 Lung-changing cigarettes,
How necessary to youth
And painful to contemplate
For the busy-bodying old!
With desperation – or so
25 Sometimes it seems to me –
I hang on to what they waste
As once I wasted it.

Somewhere I read – what confirms
My sentient life of late –
30 'Old men cry easily.'
Who would have thought I should mourn
The future of healthy louts,
The bunions of pretty girls?
The heavens sufficiently ope
35 To show the worn gold ring
Of the moon's beginning light.
Such mild observations fall
In the 'pindarics' used
By Arnold for his laments
40 Over his father, dead;
Wordsworth; the Kraut who took
So long to die in France;
And the multiple Brontës, dead.

For arraigning England he
45 Forgave Heinrich Heine – since
'We echo the blame of her foes'.
How much easier to forgive
Would Arnold find it today

When our 'glory, genius and joy'
50   Are sunk to a still lower notch!

The sparrow – commonplace, small:
Yes, that is confirmed when a bird
Hops strangely into the house.
And I cup it in my hands
55   To counter what chilling shock
Brought it to seek the help
Of those impuissant enough
In tragedies of their own.
But beautiful also the bird:
60   The eye a tiny gem
Found in a bundle of rags.
How quickly one gets to know
A fellow creature – the marks
That make each one unique
65   (Including such accidents
As a beak with adhering bread)
And even hidden traits
That the character underpin.

Next morning (as one had guessed)
70   He is dead, and I take him up –
Weightless, unwarm – to inter
Where daffodils all look south.

Moss on the paving, furred
Like caterpillars, gold on green,
75   May be removed with Jeyes
Fluid, the wiseacres say.
Another way is to run
A Dutch hoe along the cracks –
Labour of many days,
80   Dead weight of material, doomed
To the socialist compost heap.
What other sproutings, more

14

Seemly to bourgeois souls,
These winter killings succeed –
85 Lilies of brown-moled white
Throats and the velvet rose!

Winter one day, the next
Balmily Spring, I throw
The artificial green
90 Of the first mowings upon
The oddly neutral pile

Arnold would not have thought
The answer to England's ills,
Whatever it was, to be cold
95 Verse or hot Ovaltine.
Charm is what makes, he said,
The work of poets divine.
I well can understand
He would think these lines devoid
100 Of charm, stuck as they are
With the cares of a Philistine world.
Yet no one is more aware
Than I of the Beast-ruled age –
So might be thought lucky to hold
105 A 'Travel Permit For
Elderly Person' which must
In the end see one safely across
That dark and bitter stream
Beyond encircling hands
110 – Though in fact I would give it up
For another painful stay,
Cigarettes, corns and all,
On the parlous nearer shore.

Quatrains of an Elderly Man

Summer's End

A wasp starts burrowing in my naked toe,
No doubt preparatory to laying eggs.
Does it imagine I'm already dead
Or is it one that dooms a living host?

In the Night

5   I wake up, vaguely terrified, at three
And switch the light on, reach out for my book,
And slip inside the life of sanity
Of Wopsle, Gargery and Pumblechook.

South-East London

I witnessed the disappearance of the tram,
10 The trolley-buses' rise and fall, but who'd
Have thought to see a change of climate come –
Hefty black schoolgirls in the Old Kent Road?

Low Tide at Greenwich

BEWARE OF CRANES (it says) but all I see
Are swans at the river's edge, past rusty wrecks
15 Of piles and barges, preening on polished mud
Their dazzling hulls with dislocated necks.

Listening

I still can tell from high fidelity,
Thank God, low ditto: yet who cares how thin,
When certain cadences get under way,
20 The fossil baritone or violin?

Writing

What verses, even now, I judge I write!
– Almost as decent as I hope they'll be.

16

These are the verses I compose at night
When booze suspends my judging faculty.

Poetry and Whist

25 How enviable Herrick's
Fourteen hundred lyrics!
– Though, as the Scot complained when they dealt him all
The trumps, a lot of them were small.

Robbed

Somewhere along the way I changed my person
30 With an old man. Where is he now, that thief?
Perhaps enjoying in my flesh exertion
Only a criminal could carry off.

Late-born Infants

His last few cycles for piano Brahms
Described as lullabies of his own sadness.
35 What marvellous things old men hold in their arms,
That sleep and wake and bring them fleeting gladness!

The Metaphysical

Donne took his propositions much as tricks
To induce belief in something really true.
Strange world, where legs are merely two straight sticks,
40 Yet flesh turns into spirit at their screw.

Dreams

It's dreams of jealousy that now give pain,
Not jealousy itself. The feeling's gone
In actual life – as well as the beauteous, vain
Possession it spied and grew viridian on.

Time

₄₅ It seems, because of inactivity,
That sombre suits, black shoes and motor-cars
Last longer. But meantime across my eye
Flickers the yearly shifting of the stars.

Ordinary Seaman

The 143ft mast of *HMS Ganges* at Shotley, Suffolk, has been listed as a
monument by the Department of the Environment – news item, 1976

Inscribe thereon that in 1941
₅₀ I climbed it twice in fright.
Once as a routine but also (to make sure
I dared) the previous night.

Winter

I step from the house at nightfall, thereby knowing
How startlingly life continues in the wild –
₅₅ Far traffic's pedal, trees very quietly growing,
The air as cool as kisses of a child.

Pacifism

Utterly strange babies offer sucks of lollies,
Like ants to aggressor ants: propitiation
Needless for me. But what more venal follies
₆₀ Will they commit when *they* form the invasion?

High Up

Pruning an apple-tree among the birds –
Each keeping nonetheless its self-judged distance –
I marvel at the spate of avian words
Through January's still unthawed resistance.

January 1977

₆₅ New Moon near Venus on the twenty-third,
The satellite's rondure underlined in fire;

Its face ambiguous in the brownish shade:
Love's tiny planet blurred as through a tear.

Kissing on the Bus

Surely I'd be as concerned about other lives
70 As about my own had I the entrée to them.
As it is, I sneer at these public youthful loves
And smugly read the obituary column.

Accident

My briefcase falls open in the street. Displayed:
Aspirins for migraine, chocolates for my wife.
75 Despite my 'Oh, bugger', strangers come to aid
The old boy picking up his bits of life.

Winter's End

Match-heads of white and ochre on the jade
Match-sticks of snowdrop and crocus; almost pink
Warty excrescences on the peach's twig:
80 And suddenly birds have time to sing and chase.

Laziness

In the June garden, as supine I lie,
An aircraft's great white loosening cable of exhaust
Blows over. Then the flawless heavens defy
The finding of emblems for a future holocaust.

19

Two

The Poet and His Art

To an Unknown Reader

You, too, are a poet, I guess, though lacking
Perhaps any public success – or even
The patience or skill to write the notation
Of your song: a private bathroom vocalist.

5 Have you thought that you may be happier thus?
Woman past youth, pottering in the dead ground
Between lunch and the return of your children,
Boy in the Pentonville of the provinces,

Ageing widow with leisure, friends fallen off –
10 Aren't your dreams better than syllable-counting,
Than a whole lifetime's remorseful exposure
Of a talent falling short of its vision?

Envious even of the present success,
Your answer will be a denial, I'm sure.
15 And if so, why then you have entered our ranks
Without need of further proof – timid haters

Of cruelty and hostilities, to whom
All history is the history of pain.
From a sharer in your weakness you'll get small
20 Reassurance, and pleasure's not my motive.

Yet you read on, having kept, like a junkie,
The text for solitude, though undoubtedly
Turning to far stronger drugs in recurring
Times of less easily relieved unhappiness.

In chambers of torture, alcoholic cats,
Chain-smoking rabbits, provide the antidotes
For the injuries inflicted by ourselves
And by the societies we have fashioned.

It's part of the character we share to fret
30 About the animals we've condemned: indeed,
What's worst to contemplate in the forthcoming
Doomsday is the extinction of their courage;

Let alone of the evolution down time
Of sonneteering rats, observant wood-lice,
35 Comparison-discovering barnacles –
Poets without fatal taint of the human.

Would you want me to end in such a forlorn
Key? I think not, for the poet is disposed
To believe the domestic bell will be rung
40 At last by the understanding stranger –

Quite against probability. And it's just
That continuing expectation of words,
Of opening portals, to promise more than they
Really signify to which man's hope adheres.

45 Alternatives to dead-ends of history
Are what's conspiratorially offered;
All verse threatening that, as the Yankee said:
'The astonished Muse finds thousands at her side.'

Jag and Hangover

I have spent some days of late
Exalted, ambitious, free,
In a stupor of poetry,
And now I open my eyes

To find without much surprise
All incurably second-rate.

The muse's visitations
Fatigue and inflame the sense,
Are precisely as intense
For McGonagalls as for Donnes:
The word appears and stuns
The power to see true relations.

When we desire to say
'Red' and our pen puts down
'Cardinal' all the crown
Of our head becomes alive,
And we imagine five
Or six continents under our sway.

Our ordinary features
Harden to some gold mask;
Like the princess' task
Assumed by dwarfs, the long
History before the song
Can be lived by the singing creatures

Is over, and the earth
Has images for matter.
But soon realities spatter
Both lines and world with dead
Areas where the head
Perceives unsowable dearth.

And so our subject resumes
The massive poverty
From which, improbably,
Tribunes deduce the elate
Harmonious future state
Of rich individual blooms.

Dialogue of the Poet and his Talent

Poet

I give you this calm, star-thick night of Spring,
A hooting owl that freezes in mid-air
The foreleg of the cat; a garden where
You may make courteous contact, like a king,
With lower life; and in the house an earth
Of anxiety and love, with some escape
Through sleep into that country of your birth
Where the desire can summon up the shape.

Talent

And these could be enough: I want to use
That almost-face, those other worlds; the small
Existences that parody the tall;
The holy family, the dream's excuse.
But I demand from you an attitude –
What Burckhardt called the Archimedean point
Outside events, perhaps – in which the crude
World and my words would marry like a joint.

Poet

How well I know your wish! It is my own.
To be committed or to stand apart:
Either would heal the wound. Alas, my heart,
Too cowardly, too cold, is always blown
By gusts of revulsion from the self and aim
Of simple man, yet sharing in his fate
It cannot calmly watch the stupid game
With the moon's irony, the orbit's state.

25 Then I must be content with images:
At worst the eye's own coloured stars and worms,
At best all the reflective mind affirms;
Wishing to people steppe, metropolis
And littoral, yet only finding room
30 To note inadequately on my pages
The senseless cataclysms of their doom;
While coiled in others sleep new words, new ages.

Dead Poet

Going across the piebald summer green,
By the glass pond, the willow's waterfall,
I wonder suddenly if I shall see you

In one of your familiar emanations –
5 With walking-stick, perhaps, or musing on
A bench of the municipality.

At once I remember you are dead. A step
More on the slippery beige and then the thought:
But shan't we soon be meeting, after all?

10 Fanciful concept, since I disbelieve
In after-life. Nor shall I join you in
Some notional pantheon of immortal bards –

Part of the irony of coming death
Is just its confirmation one's to be,
15 Despite a life of trying otherwise,

A nonentity. No doubt too late I note
That people usually choose as favourites,
Out of my poems, pieces (all too few)

On the demise of cats, or filial guilt.
It seems I rarely found the common touch,
Though my emotions common as they come.

Drawn to a tapping stick run creviced ants,
More than a hundred times as old as man.
The heart being recently invented, they

Own just a cardiac vessel. Poets sunk
Within their art ostensibly possess
Such myrmecoid heartlessness in life itself,

Yet, as one's circle, like a dish of cherries,
Gradually decreases to the tough
Or the deformed, how copious the tears!

The chairs stay out all night. Shall I get through
The shortening days to laze in them again,
And say once more: I'll savour these at least –

Make go as slowly as the gnomon's shade,
Or even stop, like green nasturtium wheels;
Spending more time out in the hedgehog's moon?

August itself has undertones of Fall,
Some inexplicable, imperial,
Elgarian sadness. Don't we long to assume,

As simply as the starling, winter plumage,
See off our final brood in mellow days,
Die stoically, and carefully out of sight?

Licking each other and exchanging food –
Is how ants spend their lives. So far as men
Swerve from that model is the measure of

Unhappiness, what makes precisely for
The human: culture of neurosis – cities
Ant-riddled from scratch, chronicled by the sky.

Poet and Reader

Your verses are depressing,
Obsessed with years and death:
Don't you observe the blessing
In merely drawing breath,
5 *In things that aren't so pressing?*

Remember, please, my verse
Comes out of moods of pleasure,
If life were any worse
There wouldn't be the leisure
10 Even to moan and curse.

The very act of warning
Implies a faith in readers:
It's not quite you I'm mourning,
Rather the seedy leaders
15 You are for ever spawning.

All art foresees a future,
Save art which fails to weigh
The sadness of the creature,
The limit of its day,
20 Its losing war with nature.

The Poet: his Public

I wrote a book for girls and boys —
Seen Grandpa Lately?
I doubt if any child enjoys
It greatly.

But several grown-ups said to me:
'It's rather good –
The first lot of your poetry
We've understood.'

Chekhov

Chekhov saw life as a series of departures;
Its crises blurred by train times, bags, galoshes.
Instead of saying the important word
The hurried characters only breathe Farewell.

And what there was of meaning in it all
Is left entirely to the minor figures:
Aged or stupid, across the deserted stage,
They carry, like a tray, the forgotten symbol.

The Two Poets

The one was witty and observant,
Words and translucent form his servant.
The other counted beats, weighed vowels,
His verse as thick and coiled as bowels.

The first died young. The second aged,
And, though officially he raged
Against the former, privately
Envied the light, lost poetry.

Envied but never ceased to hope,
Thinking it still within his scope,
That unsought carelessness and truth
– The lucky manner of his youth.

Rhetoric of a Journey

The train takes me away from the northern valleys
Where I lived my youth and where my youth lives on
In the person of my parent and the stone walls,
The dialect of love I understand
5 But scarcely speak, the mills and illnesses.

In Trollope's novel open on my knee
The characters are worried about money:
The action revolves round the right to a necklace.
I have only to bend my head and immediately
10 I am lost in this other reality, the world
Of art, where something is always missing.
In *The Eustace Diamonds* life is made tolerable
By standing away from time and refusing to write
Of the hours that link the official biography.

15 I think of the poem I wrote on another visit –
A list of the poet's hoarded perceptions:
The net of walls thrown over waves of green,
The valleys clogged with villages, the cattle
Pink against smoking mills – and only now
20 Experience what was delayed and omitted.
For those were rooms in which we dared not look
At each other's load of emotion: it was there
Our past had to die: and where we acknowledged
With pain and surprise our ties with the disregarded.
25 I would like to renounce the waking rational life,
The neat completed work, as being quite
Absurd and cowardly; and leave to posterity
The words on book-marks, enigmatic notes,
Thoughts before sleep, the vague unwritten verse
30 On people, on the city to which I travel.

I would like to resolve to live fully
In the barbarous world of sympathy and fear.

Says his life to the poet: 'Can you make verse of this?'
And the poet answers: 'Yes, it is your limitations
35 That enable me to get you down at all.'
The diamonds glitter on his paper and
His sons sail unloved to the Antipodes.
Those whom a lack of creativeness condemns
To truth see magazines in the hands of the patient
40 And realise that the serial will go on
After death; but the artist becomes ill himself.
For only the fully-committed participate
In the revolution of living, the coming to power
Of death: the others have always some excuse
45 To be absent from the shooting, to be at home
Curled up with a book or at the dentist's.

Sometimes I find it possible to feign
The accent of the past, the vulgar speech
Which snobbery and art have iced; but feel no longer
50 The compulsion of hills, the eternal interests
Which made my fathers understand each other.
That mockery of solidarity
Some of the civilized always experience,
Waiting half hopefully for the dreaded barbarians,
55 Sick of their culture, traitors to the division
Of toil and sensibility. Yet really
I can speak easily only to myself.
The tears meant for others are wept in front of the glass;
The confession is never posted; and the eye
60 Slides away from the proffered hand and discovers
An interesting view from the window.

The ridiculous mottled faces pass in stiff
Procession: relations, friends and chance encounters.
And the asinine minds that lie behind the gestures

29

65 Of goodness I can never reciprocate
Repel me with their inability
To escape from the grossest errors. Is it weakness
That sometimes imagines these shaped as heroes?
That cannot conceive of happiness as other
70 Than the apotheosis of the simple and kind?
That refuses to see how the century rises, pale,
From the death of its dream, ignoring the gains
Of the cruel, the different wishes of slaves?
The train removes me to another set
75 Of evasions. The valleys disappear. The train
Bolts through the central plain. I shall discover
Whether Lizzie Eustace retained her diamonds,
How far the hordes are from the city,
And my end will make significant for me
80 A casual place and date. My own child
Will grow from the generous warmth of his youth and
    perhaps
Discover, like me, that the solemn moments of life
Require their unbearable gaucheness translated to art.
For the guilt of being alive must be appeased
85 By the telling observation, and even feeling
Can only be borne retrospectively.
Bending over to kiss, the sensitive see with alarm
That their selves are still upright: the instant of death is
    announced
By a rattle of tin in the corridor. Meaning is given
90 These disparate happenings, our love is only
Revealed, by conventions: 'Dear Mother, I hope you are
    better.'
Or 'Lizzie resolved that she would have her revenge.'

The lilac will last a fortnight if the rain
Arrives, the sparrows will always turn to let
95 Their lime drop over the gutter, the gardener

Will lift the chickweed, and the clots of nests
In the elms disappear in the whirling green of summer.

At the end of the twilit road a figure is standing
Calling us to go in, while the far-off rumours
Of terrible facts which at last may destroy
Our happiness spoil our play. In the place we go to
The kettle boils on the fire, the brasses are polished,
But people are busy with pain in another room.
One night I shall watch the city and black sky meet
In the distance, the car lights stream on the heath like tracer,
And in such moments of lonely and mild exultation
This rhetoric will be forgotten, and the life of omission go
     on.
Behind me will lie the sad and convulsive events
As narrative art, and as fated, immortal and false.

Three
Poetry and Politics

Chinoiserie

I've always been comfortably off.
In my poorer days my desires were modest:
Now I earn more, my previous habits
Circumscribe the area of my extravagance.
I've tried to take care that being a poet
Didn't get in the way of my making a living,
And eventually this other occupation
Actually incremented my income
And stopped hurting my respectability.
It's a toss up whether I turn first
To the literary or the financial page,
And I find it just as painful to read
Of a bonus issue of shares I failed to buy
As of the success of a rival writer.
Yet I can seriously assert
That finally money doesn't matter.
It's supported a life I can't approve of:
I've saved it for a life I shall never enjoy.
Like my neatness and punctuality,
My interest in it denotes a fixation
At the irrelevant anal stage of existence.
If I became penniless tomorrow . . .
Still impossible to change to a hero of art!
An incurable lack of high seriousness
Is indicated by concern about cash;
A deficiency in the religious sense;

A fatal practicality for life.
Given this species of character,
My follies have arisen from denying it –
30 Underestimating the greed of others,
And the longevity of capitalism.
How much happier I'd have been
Had I put my patrimony in low-yielders,
And been less timid and considerate,
35 And voted Tory, and stuck to prose.

Florestan to Leonora

Our shadows fall beyond the empty cage.
The Minister has gone and I am left
To try to live with your heroic age.

I spare a thought, my dear, for you who must
5 Go home to change the jackboots for a skirt
And put the pistol on its nail to rust;

But mainly think of my impossible task.
My own love might have tried what yours achieved:
It cannot bear the gift it did not ask.

10 After the trumpet I felt, in our embrace,
I had been cheated of the captured's right
To innocent inaction and to face

A suffering unjust as a sarcoma.
Did you never conceive that it was possible
15 To like incarceration? In this trauma

Of the imprisoning era there must be
Some prisoners – for torturers to visit,
To wear the pallor and the beards of free

Philosophers, and tap on streaming walls
20 Their selfless ineffective messages
Concerning liberty to brutish cells.

When the mob sang of brotherhood and joy
I was embarrassed, more so when I saw
The near-erotic answer in your eye.

25 You take my hand as though I ought to live;
And lead me out to that alarming world
Which, the oppressor dead, the sensitive

Can find inimical no longer. Yes,
Our values must shrivel to the size of those
30 Held by a class content with happiness;

And warmed by our children, full of bread and wine,
I shall dream of the discipline of insomnia
And an art of symbols, starved and saturnine.

The Ides of March

Fireballs and thunder augment the wailing wind:
A vulgar score, but not inappropriate
To my romantic, classic situation.
Within the house my wife is asleep and dreaming
5 That I, too, am cocooned inside the world
Of love whose fear is that the other world
Will end it. But I wait uneasy here
Under the creaking trees, the low dark sky,
For the conspirators. This is the place
10 Where I come, in better weather, with a book
Or pen and paper – for I must confess
To a little amateur scribbling. Love and letters:
One ought to be content – would, if the times
Were different; if state and man were free,

The slaves fed well, and wars hung over us
Not with death's certainty but with the odds
Merely of dying a not too painful death.
Yes, I have caught the times like a disease
Whose remedy is still experimental;
20 And felt the times as some enormous gaffe
I cannot forget. And now I am about
To cease being a fellow traveller, about
To select from several complex panaceas,
Like a shy man confronted with a box
25 Of chocolates, the plainest after all.
I am aware that in my conscious wish
To rid the empire of a tyrant there
Is something that will give me personal pleasure;
That usually one's father's death occurs
30 About the time one becomes oneself a father.
These subtleties are not, I think, important –
No more than that I shall become a traitor,
Technically, to my class, my friend, my country.
No, the important thing is to remove
35 Guilt from this orchard, which is why I have
Invited here those men of action with
Their simpler motives and their naked knives.
I hope my wife will walk out of the house
While I am in their compromising presence,
40 And know that what we built had no foundation
Other than luck and my false privileged rôle
In a society that I despised.
And then society itself, aghast,
Reeling against the statue, also will
45 Be shocked to think I had a secret passion.
Though passion is, of course, not quite the word:
I merely choose what history foretells.
The dawn comes moonlike now between the trees
And silhouettes some rather muffled figures.

It is embarrassing to find oneself
Involved in this clumsy masquerade. There still
Is time to send a servant with a message:
'Brutus is not at home': time to postpone
Relief and fear. Yet, plucking nervously
55 The pregnant twigs, I stay. Good morning, comrades.

Expostulation and Inadequate Reply

I wish you would write a poem, in blank verse,
addressed to those who, in consequence of the
complete failure of the French Revolution,
have thrown up all hopes of the amelioration
of mankind, and are sinking into an almost
epicurean selfishness, disguising the same
under the soft titles of domestic attachment
and contempt for visionary philosophes. –
                          COLERIDGE to WORDSWORTH, 1799.

Alas! dear Coleridge, I am not the man,
After a century and a half, to write
That poem – of another Revolution
And yet another generation of
5   Poets who, since the age holds out no hope,
Abjure the age and its attempted changers,
Trying to find in personal love their tropes
For poetry and reason for their lives.
It will not do: their verse is sloppy and
10   Their beings trivial or meaningless.
For still the active world maintains the turn
It took when you were young, and posed against
Its harsh demands for truth and sacrifice
The useless poet must arrange himself
15   With care if he is not to be an adjunct

Reactionary or irrelevant.
Of course, my only difference is I know
How weak I am, what strength the times require:
Attempting to disown the spurious virtue
20   That springs from guilt and from the making out
Of paths I dare not tread.

                                    I wonder how
(Writing these lines beneath the gentle gold
That streams obliquely from the branches soon
25   To show entirely their essential structure)
Precisely you regarded that autumnal
World which arrived so quickly after Spring.
Could you imagine yet another chance
For tyranny to die, for men to make
30   An order of equality and right?
You did not sink, I know, immediately
Into acceptance of the status quo,
The old lies and the old injustices.
And history, although you could not tell,
35   Was gathering up the scattered elements
To make in time another grand assault
Upon the barricades of privilege,
Islands of class, the beaches of selfish atoms,
And will again, though it's our tragedy
40   – And opportunity – that history
Is only the totality of action
By many men who each alone are blind
To what they do, and may do.

                                    Seen far off
45   The forest's million bones are smudged with bands
Of bistre, raw sienna, faded green.
Sad season of the end of growth, the start
Of cold that seems, in this faint sun, will be
Unbearable! And yet it will be borne,
50   And those who can survive will find the new,

37

Delicate but sure republic of the crocus,
The warm fraternal winds, the growing strength
Of wheat and apple's equal luxury.
This could not be the poem you desired.
55 We grow to understand that words alone,
The visionary gleam through which the poet
More and more consciously, less frequently,
Renews his youth, are, like all art, condemned
To failure in the sense that they succeed.
60 You, who so early lost that power, know best
How men forever seek, not quite in vain,
Sublime societies of imagination
In worlds like this, and that no more exist.

Dedicatory Epistle with a Book of 1949

To Jack Clark and Alan Ross

Here's proof – as if one needed any –
Of Fuller's classic parsimony.
One volume, two dedicatees;
So little verse and less to please,
5 Alan, I hear you say, behind
That manner which is always kind:
'No meat, and where's the bloody gravy?
He wrote much better in the Navy'.
And you, Jack, glancing up from Proust:
10 'It's compromise come home to roost'.

Hysteria is the destiny
Of those who want, insatiably,
In childhood love; and the condition
Of being wet in bed's ambition.
15 What kind of pasts must we have led
That now we're neither red nor dead?

38

We had our fill of love and hunger
When uninhibited and younger:
After we lost the initial breast
20 We knew a falling off of zest;
And while the workless topped three million
Read Eliot in the pavilion;
For us the Reichstag burned to tones
Of Bach on hand-made gramophones;
25 We saw the long-drawn fascist trauma
In terms of the poetic drama;
And even the ensuing war
For most was something of a bore.

Dear Clark, it's you to whom I speak,
30 As one who hovered in that clique:
A wit and cause of wit in others;
Who called the working-class half-brothers;
Easy at Lords or Wigmore Hall;
A nibbler at the off-side ball –
35 We would have moved, were held, alas,
In the paralysis of class.
We spoke our thoughts not loud and bold
But whispered through the coward's cold;
And all the time, with deadly humour,
40 Inside us grew the traitor's tumour.
Nothing I say can warn, console,
You who've survived the liberal rôle,
And in a world of Camps and Bomb
Wait for the end with false aplomb.

45 The nineteenth century dream of good
Erecting barricades of wood
And storming keypoints of reaction
To substitute its kindly faction,
Until what's violent and rotten
50 Withers like warts tied round with cotton –
Such vision fades, and yet our age

39

Need not become the last blank page,
And though the future may be odd
We shouldn't let it rest with God;
55 Confused and wrong though things have gone
There is a side we can be on:
Distaste for lasting bread and peace
May thus support a king in Greece,
And trust in General Chiang Kai-shek
60 Will safely lead to freedom's wreck.

Our dreams no longer guard our sleep:
The noses of the road-drills creep,
With thoughts of death, across the lawn
Out of the swarthy urban dawn.
65 And one by one, against our will,
The cultured cities vanish till
We see with horror just ahead
The sudden end of history's thread.
Ross, with your innings' lead of years,
70 Such brooding will not bring your tears.
You lived when doom was not the fashion,
What's sad for you is human passion.
Your verse is sensuous, not spare,
Somerset in, not Lancashire.
75 We disagree in much, I know:
I'm over-fond of Uncle Joe;
You find in Auden not an era –
Simply a poet who grows queerer;
The working-class for you's a fact,
80 No statue in the final act.
Yet we should never come to blows
On this – that man as artist goes,
And in that rôle, most sane, most free,
Fulfils his spacious infancy;
85 That truth's half feeling and half style,
And feeling and no style is vile.

About us lie our elder writers,
Small, gritty, barren, like detritus:
Resistance to the epoch's rage
90   Has not survived their middle age.
The type of ivory tower varies
But all live in the caves of caries.
The younger men, not long from mother,
Write articles about each other,
95   Examining, in solemn chorus,
Ten poems or a brace of stories.
The treason of the clerks is when
They make a fetish of the pen,
Forget that art has duties to –
100   As well as to the 'I' – the 'You',
And that its source must always be
What presses most, most constantly.
Since Sarajevo there has been
Only one thing the world could mean,
105   And each successive crisis shows
That meaning plainer than a nose.
Sassoon found Georgian style napoo
To state what he was going through:
And Owen knew why he was born –
110   To write the truth and thus to warn.
The poet now must put verse back
Time and again upon the track
That first was cut by Wordsworth when
He said that verse was meant for men,
115   And ought to speak on all occasions
In language which has no evasions.

Dear friends, I wish this book bore out
More than the bourgeois' fear and doubt.
Alas, my talent and my way
120   Of life are useless for today.
I might have cut a better figure

41

When peace was longer, incomes bigger.
The 'nineties would have seen me thrive,
Dyspeptic, bookish, half-alive.
125 Even between the wars I might
With luck have written something bright.
But now, I feel, the 'thirties gone,
The dim light's out that could have shone.
My richest ambiguity
130 Is nightmares now, not poetry:
After eight lines the latter ends
Unless I'm babbling to my friends.
The arteries and treaties harden,
The shadow falls across the garden,
135 And down the tunnel of the years
The spectre that we feared appears.
Gazing upon our love or book,
Between the lines or in the look,
We see that choice must fall at last,
140 And the immortal, lucky past –
Thinking of bed or lying in it –
Cry out and crumble in a minute.
For such times are these poems meant,
A muted, sparse accompaniment,
145 Until the Wagner we await
Provides a score that's up to date,
And world and way and godheads pass
To vulgar but triumphant brass.

Translation

Now that the barbarians have got as far as Picra,
And all the new music is written in the twelve-tone scale,
And I am anyway approaching my fortieth birthday,
       I will dissemble no longer.

5   I will stop expressing my belief in the rosy
Future of man, and accept the evidence
Of a couple of wretched wars and innumerable
       Abortive revolutions.

I will cease to blame the stupidity of the slaves
10 Upon their masters and nurture, and will say,
Plainly, that they are enemies to culture,
       Advancement and cleanliness.

From progressive organisations, from quarterlies
Devoted to daring verse, from membership of
15 Committees, from letters of various protest
       I shall withdraw forthwith.

When they call me reactionary I shall smile,
Secure in another dimension. When they say
'Cinna has ceased to matter' I shall know
20   How well I reflect the times.

The ruling class will think I am on their side
And make friendly overtures, but I shall retire
To the side farther from Picra and write some poems
       About the doom of the whole boiling.

25 Anyone happy in this age and place
Is daft or corrupt. Better to abdicate
From a material and spiritual terrain
       Fit only for barbarians.

To George Woodcock, in his and the Author's Sixty-fifth Year

What Marxian spectre lays its beard on the evening?

Lettere dal carcere: yes, but all
Our letters come from prison. In latter days
I'm reading this book by Gramsci, not for ways

To overthrow the wicked bourgeoisie,
5 Merely to pick up hints for comprehending
Life from a locked-up hunchback's ponderings.

Long since, in war-time, you opposed the war-god --
A stance not quite uncomical. Though now
I might well think: how right! But then it seemed

10 Evil would only go through evil done.
Besides, the issued arms might in the end
Save us from right-wing maniacs of our own.

As for the past (ongoing!) life of art,
We surely would have never disagreed
15 On Seneca's epistolary advice:

'Avoid shabby attire, long hair, an unkempt beard;
A known antipathy to knives and forks;
Sleeping on floors; and other misguided means

Of self-advertisement.' I move from book
20 To tape, the longest trek that, ageing, I want
To take (and you yourself have somewhat cut

Your literally Pacific voyagings);
Hear music that recalls a time before
You and I'd even met: green then my age!

25 The pianist of that date a friend whose death
Alone proved he'd become more dear: the fiddler,

44

Widowered, gassed himself at once – odd fate

For someone utterly *moyen sensuel*,
Although response to Bruch's *schmalz* (our own
30   Not least) must always put us on our guard.

I tie together time and death and art;
Marvel how close to sentimentality
Is art's essential – lasting melody.

O fiddler, dead in what we'd now regard
35   As youth! O friend, whose age at death we've passed!
In our last decade what fresh insights grow!

From the jail I, and even you, escaped,
Gramsci (about the parcels sent from home)
Complained he didn't get the Cirio

40   ('A brand of marmalade' explains the note).
The nearer we come to losing them, the more
Precious and meaningful the trivia,

So called, of life. The more prolonged the span
Of consciousness the greater homage due
45   Its fragile vehicle: to cheer the one

Who's lived so long – still more, his friends – by marking
Odd-numbered lustra, wishing him enough
(And lasting) liberty and marmalade;

Fighting to get them if we're also tough.
50   Gramsci in jail's like us at sixty-five.
'No point in having a new suit made for Court.

'After I'm sentenced I'll be issued with
A proper prisoner's outfit – tunic below
Shaved head. But I agree that folk might say

55   'My ancient jacket at the trial was
For demogogic show, and so I'll wear
The decent suit I'd kept "for best".' The suit

You and I keep for death and anniversaries.

45

Obituary of R. Fuller

We note the death, with small regret,
Of one who'd scarcely lived, as yet.
Born just before the First World War,
Died when there'd only been one more:
5   Between, his life had all been spent
In the small-bourgeois element,
Sheltered from poverty and hurt,
From passion, tragedy and dirt.
His infant traumas somewhat worse,
10   He would have written better verse,
His youth by prudence not so guided
His politics been more decided.
In the event his life was split
And half was lost bewailing it:
15   Part managerial, part poetic –
Hard to decide the more pathetic.
Avoiding China, Spain and Greece,
He passed his adult years of peace
In safe unease, with thoughts of doom
20   (As birth is feared inside the womb) –
Doom of his talent and his place,
Doom, total, of the human race.
This strange concern for fellow creatures
Had certainly some pathic features.
25   He could not understand that death
Must be the lot of all with breath,
And crudely linked felicity
With dying from senile decay,
Finding no spiritual worth
30   In guided missiles, torture, dearth.
Quite often he was heard to babble
'Poets should be intelligible'

Or 'What determines human fate
Is the class structure of the state'
Or 'Freud and Marx and Dickens found –
And so do I – souls not profound'.
These views were logically a feature
Of his rude, egotistic nature –
So unemotional and shy
Such friends as he retained would cry
With baffled boredom, thankful they
Were not part of his family.

If any bit of him survives
It will be that verse which contrives
To speak in private symbols for
The peaceful caught in public war.
For there his wavering faith in man
Wavers around some sort of plan,
And though foreseeing years of trouble,
Denies a universal rubble,
Discovering in wog and sailor
The presages of bourgeois failure.
Whether at this we weep or laugh
It makes a generous epitaph.

Four

War

First Air-Raids

Not the moon's light —
Theatrical mauve,
Antiquing the city —
Nor winging danger
5 Nor guns in the grove,
Strange in the night,
Add beauty to anger;

But my undismayed
Pouring of love
10 In the crouching city
While things more certain
Than Hamlet's glove
Round reckless blade
Strike through the curtain.

15 Only when that dies
In sewers and streets
Will guns in the city
Fade with history;
Since love completes
20 Fear and is cries
For what can't be.

London Air-raid, 1940

An ambulance bell rings in the dark among
The rasp of guns, and abstract wrong is brought
Straight to my riveted thought.

Tonight humanity is trapped in evil
5   Pervasive as plague or devil; hopelessly wages
With pain, like the Middle ages.

My reading and the alimentary city
Freeze: crouching fear and licking pity's all
Of the handed animal.

Battersea: after Dunkirk, June 3 1940

Smoke corrugated on the steel-blue sky
From the red funnels of the power-station
Is blanched as the shocking bandages one sees
On soldiers in the halted train. Patience!
5   Still there is nothing definite to say —
Or do, except to watch disintegration,
The rightness of the previous diagnosis,
And guard oneself from pity and isolation.

The generator's titanic vessel floats
10   Beside the Thames; and smoke continues to pour.
Khaki and white move on as though to hide
In summer. What can keep the autumn fates
From breaking the perfect sky and sending power
For slaves to set against the pyramid?

The Phoney War

Sitting at home and reading Julien Benda;
Evening descending in successive gauzes –
Pantomime transformation scene reversed;
A point releasing Haydn from a groove
In waves alternately severe and tender:

A curious way to spend a night of war!

Though more and more clearly I see my bona-fides.
Under the growing pressure of the mould
I'm now compact, one of the very small
And disillusioned poets of the era;
Soothsayers who lived on into the Ides.

So action or avowal would be pretence.
Not that I now may draw back from the edge –
The threat of being pushed into real life
(Or realer death) – or even want to. Nor
Deny the times' need for handbooks of defiance.

Is it a lack or growth, this emollient lotion
Of words that keeps me sitting through the dusk,
To find in the martins' squeaking something sure
But vague to praise? This Frenchman says that war
Intensifies the craving for emotion.

He may be right. My own, however, shows
As an increasing fondness for Henry James;
And, if I crave at all, I crave that blight
Shall crumple less millions than thought possible,
And that on those I love shall fall few blows.

A curious war to bequeath me such a night!

Waiting to be Drafted

It might be any evening of spring;
The air is level, twilight in a moment
Will walk behind us and his shadow
       Fall cold across our day.

5   The usual trees surround an empty field
And evergreens and gravel frame the house;
Primroses lie like tickets on the ground;
       The mauve island floats on grey.

My senses are too sharp for what the mind
10   Presents them. In this common scene reside
Small elements with power to agitate
       And move me like a play.

I have watched a young stray dog with an affection
Of the eyes, and seen it peer from the encrusted
15   Lids, like a man, before it ran towards me,
       Unreasonably gay.

And watched it gnawing at a scrap of leather
In its hunger, and afterwards lying down,
Its ineffectual paws against its cracks
20   Of eyes, as though to pray.

Pity and love one instant and the next
Disgust, and constantly the sense of time
Retreating, leaving events like traps: I feel
       This always, most today.

25   My comrades are in the house, their bodies are
At the mercy of time, their minds are nothing but yearning.
From windows where they lie, as from quiet water,
       The light is taken away.

Y.M.C.A. Writing Room

A map of the world is on the wall: its lying
Order and compression shadow these bent heads.
Here we try to preserve communications;
The map mocks us with its dangerous blues and reds.

5 Today my friends were drafted; they are about
To be exploded, to be scattered over
That coloured square which in reality
Is a series of scenes, is boredom, cover,

Nostalgia, labour, death. They will explore
10 Minutely particular deserts, seas and reefs,
Invest a thousand backcloths with their moods,
And all will carry, like a cancer, grief.

In England at this moment the skies contain
Ellipses of birds within their infinite planes,
15 At night the ragged patterns of the stars;
And distant trees are like the branching veins

Of an anatomical chart: as menacing
As pistols the levelled twigs present their buds.
They have exchanged for this illusion of danger
20 The ordeal of walking in the sacred wood.

The season cannot warm them nor art console.
These words are false as the returning Spring
From which this March, history has made subtraction:
The spirit has gone and left the marble thing.

Epitaphs for Soldiers

I

Passing soldier stop and think
I was once as sad as you,
Saw in history a brink
More fearful than a bayonet's blue
5   – And left to what I thought but birds
The human message of these words.

II

Incredibly I lasted out a war,
Survived the unnatural, enormous danger
Of each enormous day. And so befell
10   A peril more enormous and still stranger:
The death by nature, chanceless, credible.

During a Bombardment by V-Weapons

The little noises of the house:
Drippings between the slates and ceiling;
From the electric fire's cooling,
Tickings; the dry feet of a mouse:
5   These at the ending of a war
Have power to alarm me more
Than the ridiculous detonations
Outside the gently coughing curtains.

And, love, I see your pallor bears
10 A far more pointed threat than steel.
Now all the permanent and real
Furies are settling in upstairs.

Memories of War

Tonight dreams may be had
(To take an instance of my own conceits)
About the one-legged dancers of the Chad.

But now the unromantic dominates.
5   From the long ward beyond my little room
Come uninhibited sounds, among them groans.

As well as farting, men could be dying there.
The feeling of a war-time mess returns
So strongly as to occasion more alarm

10   Than that tomorrow's probing will reveal
Malignancy implanted deep within.
Even the music in the ear-phones tritely

Augments the sense of thirty years ago.
Dear comrades, now we well may have to die,
15   Our span being up or proximately up.

But youth can be kept from the conscripted ranks
That trail the alleyways between the beds
And lie awake or half-asleep on beds

At doom's grossly lessened odds.

Confrontation off Korea, 1968

Return our boat that you've
Pinched from our serious play
Or with another toy
We'll roast you alive.

I pray that any nuclear war
Will be deferred till after the
Diminutive requirement for
My coming book of poesy.

The captured will confess,
Their captors arraigned. Believe
Me, both will fry unless
Tumour or clot reprieve.

The Times like a shameful secret in my case,
I pass a grinning brace
Of nymphets on their way to learning. Are
Then, you Earthman, to endure?

I wake at some ungodly hour
And fearfulness floods back. I try
The switch. Surprisingly, the power
Still sends its intricate reply.

Old order, twice before this I
Have watched your so-called death-pangs. Why
Can't one or other of us be
Put out of our misery?

Civilization has bred
A species absurd – the timid;
Which additionally is at
The terror of not surviving it.

Is the crisis to pass, then,
In the anticlimax of relief,

As a nagging pain
Proves an unmalignant spoof?

And how to enjoy the luxury
Of reprieve, we essentially
35 Condemned? Through the jokes of art,
Children's tragedy-shaped start?

Five

The Poet of Everyday Life

Fathers

My father may be often in my dreams
Yet (since he died when I was young) play parts –
Or be himself – and stay unrecognized.

In any case dreaming often modifies
5   The features of the characters we know,
Though usually telling us who's really meant,

Like useful footnotes to an allegory.
This morning speckled foam fell in the basin:
Watching my father shave came flooding back

10   From over fifty years. His cut-throat razor,
Black beard, seemed things of fascinated love –
And now replace the visage and his speech.

Did he imagine (as I sometimes do)
His son would one day reach the age of sixty,
15   Himself being almost *ipso facto* dead?

Worse, in his final illness did he think
How he would leave a foolish child of eight,
Himself being hardly out of folly's years?

The Card-table

Today it spends its life against a wall:
Facilities inside quite unemployed.
Its top can be unfolded and a leg

Swung round to make a battlefield of baize
With shallow cups to hold one's cash or chips
And zinc-based corner circlets for the drinks.

It comes down from my father and my youth.
Round it sat Issy Gotcliffe and the Weinbergs,
Powers in the textile trade in Manchester.

There I first stole an aromatic sip
Of scotch, midst laughs at my precocity:
Could be the last year of the First World War.

World vanished, almost in the mind as well –
Too young, my brother, to remember it.
All, save we supernumeraries, dead.

What point or virtue in remembering it?
Except to make it stand for everyone's
Possession of such a world – and of their loss.

The bearded faces carved upon the table's
Thighs (so to speak) will quite soon start to mean
Part of his childhood to another child.

His father will have had the enterprise
To lay out cash for art – extravagance
Condoned by delight and use, as ought to be.

My album of those days reveals that Issy
Served in the infantry – maybe in fact
He perished there, for all is speculative

In my recall, I'm sure; as history is.
At any rate, perhaps he never knew

How fascists tried to exterminate his kind.

Even in '18 he of course looked back
To times astoundingly myself had glimpsed –
A general peace, long days, illusive art.

'*Komm in den kleinen Pavillon,*' they sang –
35 Of *décor* amateurs would now reject:
Their heroes walrused; stout *grisettes*; and gay

Ill-fitting uniforms, to be exchanged
In a few years for real ones of field-grey.
Ah, music, not made cynical by Weill;

40 Love innocent in art and so in life;
Empires not cruel save through carelessness;
Summers of mere manoeuvres, courts of cards!

Family Matters

I. m. John Broadbent: ob. 3. ix. 1973

One of my mother's younger brothers dies:
My mother dead, my own age sixty-one.
The news originates in my native north.

Widowered, living in a small hotel,
5 He failed to wake today. He might have thought,
Going to bed, to amend some work of art –

Too late. Though I believe he'd not kept up
His talent as a water-colourist –
Making his mark as spare-time Thespian.

10 A mile from here one might, if one so wished,
Into the urban Thames expectorate.
It strikes me that I'm very far from home;

Yet this is where I've lived most of my life.

59

A sorrowing infant on the Pennine moors,
The borderer became a natural exile.

Or is it class that makes me sceptical:
Descendant of bloody-minded NCOs,
And probably reluctant patriots

Even in the Wars of the Roses? Yet from you –
Ironic, emotion-hiding distaff side –
Comes the true joy of life, creativeness.

Mysterious paternal ancestors,
I have to put you second in my life
To those who must have engineered my soul –

Soloists in *Elijah*, councillors
In local government, heroes of the sub-plot,
Parodists and analysts of tragic life.

How dark the trees grow when, the sun gone down,
I sit on in the young September's dusk
Until invisible against the west

The tiny flies, until a late bird soars
Too swiftly past to be identified,
Until the owl's repeated painful creak

Replaces all day's noises, and I can't
Quite see to write. One only has to choose
A different milieu for one's garden chair

Or just stay till an unfamiliar hour,
And life seems changed somehow – 'prolonged' would be
The word had not the thought come to me now

That last night, too, my uncle might have seen
Clouds first illumined by an orange light
Then disappear, the sky turn oyster grey;

The acacia leaves suspend themselves in black
And graduated brushstrokes either side
Of stems so slender as to be invisible.

Cats

(From Baudelaire)

Lovers and austere dons are equally
(In their maturity) attached to cats –
Cats soft but cruel, emperors of flats,
Touchy like these and like those sedentary.

5   Friends of the sensual, the cerebral,
They seek the quiet and horror of the dark;
If they had ever bent their pride to work
They might have pulled the funeral cars of hell.

Asleep they take the noble attitude
10 Of the great sphinxes that appear to brood,
Stretched in the wastes, in dreams that have no end;

Their loins are electric with fecundity,
And particles of gold, like finest sand,
Star vaguely their unfathomable eye.

The Family Cat

This cat was bought upon the day
That marked the Japanese defeat;
He was anonymous and gay,
But timorous and not discreet.

5   Although three years have gone, he shows
Fresh sides of his uneven mind:
To us – fond, lenient – he grows
Still more eccentric and defined.

He is a grey, white-chested cat,
10 And barred with black along the grey;

Not large, and the reverse of fat,
His profile good from either way.

The poet buys especial fish,
Which is made ready by his wife;
The poet's son holds out the dish:
They thus maintain the creature's life.

It's not his anniversary
Alone that's his significance:
In any case mortality
May not be thought of in his presence.

For brief as are our lives, more brief
Exist. Our stroking hides the bones,
Which none the less cry out in grief
Beneath the mocking, loving tones.

In Memory of my Cat, Domino: 1951–66

Rising at dawn to pee, I thought I saw you
Curved in a chair, with head raised to look at me,
As you did at such hours. But the next moment,
More used to the gloom, there was only a jar
And a face-cloth. Time enough, nonetheless,
For love's responsibilities to return
To me.
             The unique character of the dead
Is the source of our sense of mourning and loss;
So, back in bed, I avoided calling up
What I know is intact in mind, your life,
Entirely possessed as it was by my care.

I could conceive you not as dead but merely
Gone before me to a world that sends to us
Decreasing intimations of its beings –

No doubt because they find us in the end
Pathetic, worthy, but of small importance.

So long had we been together it never
Occurred to me I might fall somewhat behind.
20 Even when, familiar fur in my hands,
The sickly wave of barbiturate rose up,
I thought it was I who was journeying on –
But looking back there is only emptiness,
Your dusty medicaments and my portrait
25 Taken with you: sad mode of life you've outpaced.

More about Tompkins

One evening Tompkins' 'Mummy' calls –
    Lady two doors away.
Have we seen Tompkins anywhere?
    – Missing for all that day,
5   Yet never known to stray.

Always most punctual for his meals
    And, if abroad at night,
Letting himself into the house
    Usually by earliest light;
10   And never known to fight.

His Mummy looks me in the eye
    And sees into my mind,
She says, of course he's now too old
    To catch the avian kind –
15   Too slow, perhaps too blind.

She knows (in fact, she tells me that
    She lately read the same)
I wrote a verse about her cat –

63

His cruel, sneaky game –
20   Mentioning him by name.

By 'game' I mean his creeping through
        The shrubs on slow-motion paws,
Low as a snake, to pounce upon
        Sparrows and doves and daws
25   With murderous teeth and claws.

I shout at him, I clap my hands,
        Whenever he's around.
He still seems capable to me
        Of making a sudden bound,
30   Causing a mortal wound.

I say: 'I saw him yesterday' –
        Don't add that probably
He chattered at me from the wall
        (Spying the enemy
35   Who foils his villainy),

And that I gnash my teeth at *him*.
        I'd then been gardening, thus
The shed-door was ajar. So now,
        Feeling ridiculous,
40   I open it, call out: 'Puss!'

His Mummy adds in her own tones
        Words much more intimate.
I see among the rakes and spades
        An old soft trilby hat,
45   Nothing else like a cat.

I never had the car out, so
        No point in looking where
My Daimler lives – an object which,
        Like Tompkins, doth (I fear)
50   Oft in my verse appear.

Scarcely had Tompkins' Mummy gone,
    When back she came. And said
She'd been inspired by me to look
    In her own garden-shed,
55   And the given-up-for-dead –

Tompkins, no less – had run out, cross,
    Straight to his waiting food;
Typically, stopping not to give
    Thanks to some clever god
60   For this miraculous good.

'He'd been in there all night and day' –
    Bright was his Mummy's eye.
Strangely, a lump came in my throat
For one who used to get my goat.
65   In future, then, will my
    Foes frolic freely by?

Nino, the Wonder Dog

A dog emerges from the flies
    Balanced upon a ball.
Our entertainment is the fear
    Or hope the dog will fall.

5   It comes and goes on larger spheres,
    And then walks on and halts
In the centre of the stage and turns
    Two or three somersaults.

The curtains descend upon the act.
10   After a proper pause
The dog comes out between them to
    Receive its last applause.

Most mouths are set in pitying smiles,
　　Few eyes are free from rheum:
The sensitive are filled with thoughts
　　Of death and love and doom.

No doubt behind this ugly dog,
　　Frail, fairly small, and white,
Stands some beneficent protector,
　　Some life outside the night.

But this is not apparent as
　　It goes, in the glare alone,
Through what it must to serve absurd-
　　ities beyond its own.

Road Safety

'Watch my behind not hers.' Yes, I can just read
The insolent and meant to be witty plate
On the car in front – wearing my spectacles,
Of course, and by gum it confirms what I have
Often thought: I shall crash looking at a girl,
Like some mad three-badge stoker choked by his own
Crapulous vomit. But as soon as I vow
To myself to mend my ludicrous habits
The thought arises of inexhaustible
Generations achieving the age of eye-
Catching nubility. Die happy, old boy,
If you can at all contrive to die before
The malignancies of flesh and of the State
Gouge out the gazing and its bonanza mine.

Crisis

O courteous ladies of the West Countree!
Visiting Plymouth for the BBC,
I saw in Debenham & Freebody

'Trousers reduced'. And marched into the store –
Trousers sardined in stands upon the floor,
Trousers that won the West, that Oxford wore.

Wanting a pair to work in in the garden,
Before inflating prices further harden,
I laughingly begged the shop assistant's pardon

And asked her if among the azure jeans –
Although a style intended for the teens
Or certainly especially for the lean –

Something might fit one rather broadly-based,
An ageing man, a man without much waist.
'I'm sure there is,' she said, quite poker-faced.

And added: 'Do you know his measurements?'
Dear lady, how experienced with gents!
I meant myself. You twigged. And so I went

Smugly across the Hoe to my hotel,
Pants in a carrier. Against the hell
Of sunset the statue of the admiral

Looked out to Cadiz or the Spanish Main.
On seas courageous and in shops urbane,
Surely our England must be great again.

On the Mountain

I

Why red, why red? I ask myself, observing
A girl's enamelled nails, not understanding
The convention – an unrealistic art.

I live in a suburb of the capital,
A hill of villas, and sometimes note such things;
Old enough to remember better days.

The stoics have virtually disappeared.
I like to think myself the last of them,
Shaken but not devoured by ghastly omens.

The theatres are given up to leg shows
And gladiatorial games. The savage beasts
Are weary with the number of their victims.

In poetry the last trace of conviction
Has long since been extinguished. Round the temples
Are crowds of flautists, eunuchs and raving females.

The decoration of the baths and other
Edifices of importance is assigned
To those same careless slaves who mix the mortar.

The so-called educated classes share
The superstitions and amusements of
The vulgar, gawping at guts and moaning singers.

Atrocious taxes to 'defend' the frontiers;
Fixing maximum prices yet deploring the black market
– These the preoccupations of the state.

And the alarming aspect of imperial
Succession! The imperial madness! O
My country, how long shall we bear such things?

I find a little comfort in recalling

68

That complaints of evil times are found in every
30 Age which has left a literature behind:

And that the lyric is always capable
Of rejuvenation (as is the human heart),
Even in times of general wretchedness.

II

In my garden, at the risk of annoying my cat,
35 I rescue a fledgling: as it squeaks, I see
That its tongue is like something inside a watch.

They would not find it odd, those Others –
Mysterious community, not outside
And not within the borders of the empire;

40 Not the barbarians precisely nor
The slaves: indeed, from their strange treason no
Mind is exempt . . . even the emperor's!

Could I believe? Surrender to the future,
The inevitability of the future – which
45 Nevertheless can only come by martyrdom?

Respect those priestly leaders, arguing
Whether the Second Person of the Three
Is equal or subordinate to the First?

While in their guarded monasteries they lift
50 Their greasy cassocks to ecstatic girls –
Under the bed their secret box of coin.

I suppose their creed must conquer in the end
Because it gives the simplest and most complete
Answer to all men ask in these bad years.

55 Is there a life beyond this life? Must art
Be the maidservant of morality?
And will the humble triumph? Yes. Yes. Yes.

Disgusting questions, horrible reply;
Deplorable the course of history:
60 And yet we cannot but regard with awe

The struggle of the locked and rival systems,
Involving the entire geography
Of the known world, through epochs staggeringly pro-
    longed.

To name our cities after poets, or
65 To hasten the destruction of the species –
The debate continues chronic and unresolved.

III

How rapidly one's thoughts get out of hand!
With my unsatisfactory physique
I watch the blossom through the blinding rain,

70 Cringe the while at the shoddy workmanship
Of the piddling gutter – typical of the times –
And stroke with skeleton hand the mortal fur.

It is as hard to realize where we are
As for the climber on the famous peak
75 For whom the familiar outline is no more

The record of a deadly illness or
The tearing organs of a bird of prey
But merely boredom, breathing, prudence, stones.

Happiness

Some say this is a golden age,
That never again
Will there be such a deal to eat,
Such space between the race of men.

My day's benign routines incline
To such belief
However startling, since it's sure
In time (and more than likely brief)

One will awaken not to eggs,
And isolation
In gardens, but a bed of crowding
Visitors, and emaciation.

End of the Cheap Food Era

I check my meagre purchases to see
How the enormous total has been reached.
The culprit is a pound of sausages.

Admittedly, they're Marks and Spencer's best,
Said to be 'over 90% pure pork':
Still, they're a somewhat novel luxury.

We always vowed the revolution would
Arrive when life became intolerable –
Which term we might well have envisaged as

The prospect of not affording sausages.

Oxford Album

My footfalls faintly sag the eroded stair.
Through a strait gate the garden of the Fellows.
The awesome line of tenants of the Chair.
March's male sparrows black-faced as Othellos.

The coloured scutcheons of the founding earls
Dim libraries of brown or golden hair.

71

The dreams of dons are dwarfs and little girls.
My breath augments the whited valley air.

Should time condemn the passionate to be
Oblates of culture in culture's disrepair,
Here will they raise the mocking effigy
Of emperors who deployed the ironware.

If lions may be said to live in yellows
That hue pervades the fenestrated twirls.
Youth pulses through the strangled artery
And knowledge tries to fascinate the fair.

Books and Discs

For Eric Walter White on his 75th birthday

Prokoviev by Prokoviev –
Among a clutch of photographs,
One showing the portly Glazounov
Standing beside a small piano
At which a female child is seated,
Fingers correctly bent on the keyboard,
Straight parting, hair hanging down her back,
Regular profile, far-away look –
Image asexual though erotic
(At least for those of a certain age).
This is Irene Eneri,
Captioned 'A young girl composer' –
She must look now worse than Glazounov then;
Her music even less well-known.
Later, I hear some other music say:
'Bounteous nature never never
Never feels decay.'

The Night Sky in August 1980

(with acknowledgements to *The Times* Astronomical Correspondent)

Since it was 1862 last seen,
Comet Swift-Tuttle can be expected soon.
One hundred and twenty years its period:
Tuttle and Swift by definition dead.

5 Shall I, by falling down that awkward crack,
Myself miss viewing it? Along its track,
Meanwhile, its scattered 'bits and pieces' give
Their 'annual display'. And I'm alive.

The Perseid meteors, too, are in the air.
10 Get warm and comfortable in a chair
Facing north-east, and still aspire to sight
Things to astound one in a summer night.

Abbas

Speculations

I buy the Penguin Sherlock Holmes. What wealth!
Nearly twelve hundred largish small-print pages.
I wonder what its ownership presages:
A lingering death-bed or fresh years of health?

Why

5 The felled tree doesn't know it's dead,
And sends out baby fists of leaves.
Only the obedient headsman grieves
For what superfluously bled.

Conjunctions

Fossilized urchin on the ledge that hides
10   Devices playing contrapuntal Brahms.
The captain levelly driving nuclear arms
Under a sea that towers and greenly glides.

Poets

We hate our countenances as we hate
Our verses, only by fits and starts. What bad
15   Lines career down the white, yet somehow add
A meaning to annihilating fate!

The Eighteenth Century

Announcer: 'Haydn was about thirty-nine
When he wrote this work.' So much for the 'Papa' bit.
Then follows *Sturm und Drang*; at least, as it
20   Sounded in times of mine and counter-mine.

More From the Radio

Schoenberg: 'Six Little Pieces. Opus 19.'
'Feeble Debussy,' I think, in my armchair –
Writing, or hoping that the ambient air
Inspires me to write, the wholly unforeseen.

Girls

25   Dangerous theme: bus-boarding schoolgirls. Rapt
The observer, with his aged person's card.
What follows? Pierced ears – ears! – deplored. Teeth hard
In setting pink as plastic, and more apt.

Granados

The Maiden and the Nightingale kept coming
30   Into his work. If one is to elude
The pain of unpossessable girlhood,
Beware the tell-tale brown bird's thrumming.

Christmas Eve

We are in bed. The fireplace opposite our station
Emits a bulky figure, and I'm terrified,
35 And wake myself. Interpretation: can't decide.
Your father? Mine? My infancy? Your defloration?

Old Man Feeding Birds (1)

The sparrows positively click when eating bread.
Better arrangement to possess a beak,
I think. Though duly thankful I can speak,
40 I'm more and more aware of gaps inside my head.

Old Man Feeding Birds (2)

I like to single out the crippled kind.
Of sparrows, her I dub the Tailless Wonder;
And him with crumpled claw. Whether a blunder
Of genes, or of luck in life, I do not mind.

Contemporary Music (1)

45 What if he proved a Wagner, finally!
– It strikes me, reading of a monster work
By the no longer young, perennial Turk.
What if I'd been misled by that mad eye!

Contemporary Music (2)

Forster observed: the vice of a vulgar mind
50 Is to be thrilled by bigness. Steering clear
Of something for choirs, and tapes, and other gear,
Quite reassuring to think oneself refined.

Simultaneous Games

It seems my grand-daughter made the grandmaster ponder.
Encountering (in the world of stale beginnings,
55 Analysed endings, and expected winnings)
The face and mind of twelve-years-old, no wonder!

Dreaming

What genius changes in the dream
Overheard coughs to chords of brass?
The waking talent cannot guess
The sound of things that only seem.

Strange Journey

The monstrous fare asked on a New York bus
Is sixty dollars. Through the rotting floor
Comes a great spider a woman kills. Much more . . .
I wake, and can't but admire my genius.

To a Moth

My cupped hands holding you, I awkwardly
With one elbow work the handle of the door –
Though maybe to live and die indoors was your
Proper and even happier destiny.

The Double Vase

I like a vase made like a hand
That holds aloft a flower vase
Much more than other flower jars.
But why, I fail to understand.

Early May

Tree of Spring leaves, and rain!
As though a ghost were there
Descending a rickety stair,
The showers start again.

The Wild Garden

The foxes seem to have been shot or gassed;
No longer at dusk the weighted tail, pared mask.
But am I not thankful that the daily task
Of dining foxes now is in the past?

Grand Hotel, Midnight

I'm wakened by artillery fire –
Guests slamming locks on various floors.
But what can have disturbed, outdoors,
That gull, scaringly human crier?

The Monster

85 Summer: a moth of ordinary size
Lands on some spouter on the TV screen.
When later I saw it on the prairie green
I knew why he dared not brush it from his eyes.

My Autobiography

I rather hope the memoirs of such a bloke
90 (Spasmodically attempting to be witty)
May prove that worth is creativeness and pity.
More likely that, wit failing, life's a joke.

Six

Nature

Pictures of Winter

Whips, river systems, hands of mandarins –
With trees on skies the inventive mood begins.

After the gallery's rich, vivid hoard
The still, grey river stabs me with its sword.

5   Behind the city the unmoving west
Burns smoky-orange like a robin's breast.

At four o'clock the living-room window frames
A faded photograph of roofs and flames.

Stepping outside the muffled house I freeze
10 Beneath calm, radiant immensities.

In the cold air the breath clouds of a horse
Fade, whiten, fed by two cones from their source.

Under my feet the snow cries out like mice,
Its feathers left behind compressed to ice.

15 Night, and the snow descending on the high
Branches now scarcely darker than the sky.

Décor of wolves and puppets, swans and dreams –
A snow-hung garden in a street-lamp's beams.

Closing the curtains, through the yellow light
20 I see a whiteness where it should be night.

The tangerine belies its glowing form,
But shivering bodies find each other warm.

Strange this new colour of the world I know;
Strange as my ginger cat upon the snow.

25 A general weeping from boughs still severe
Moves the heart with the turning hemisphere.

The puffed white blossom in the garden urn
Dissolves to earth that holds a queen's return.

I dig the soil and in its barren cold
30 Surprise a bulb-bomb fused with palest gold.

But still the knouts and veins divide the air,
Save for their swelling buds of sparrows, bare.

Winter Solstice

December's early-ending but forbearant days
Produce long bands of bird-egg blue or primrose skies
Divided by angry greys

That threaten to annex the total heavens – though
5 Rather surprisingly time's left for birds to fly
And even in a tree

Linger and if they're blackbirds play their xylophones.
Premature duskiness makes sparrows sharp as wrens.
Then when the day looks gone

10 The robin's rattle sounds from seeming birdless boughs.
What am I doing in this world of Georgian verse,
That carries sanguine news?

Hedge-sparrows and House-sparrows

Our medieval fathers simply named
All small birds sparrows. Hence the absurdity
Of calling these March strangers to the garden
Hedge-sparrows. Bills not the pyramids required
5   For seed-cracking, chassis altogether longer,
More Italianate, and striped along the back,
This couple trill as constantly as late
Beethoven, restless in trees, and skimming to the border.

I read, you nest in April. Stay till then
10 And populate our homely area
With dashing aviators, tireless songsters.
But how will you survive the silent hedge-cats
Consoling, too, mankind's suburban life;
Find nourishment, in face of chemical
15 Warfare against our little green invaders?
I hope my welcome's not as treacherous as Cawdor's.

No wonder that the name's a term of endearment –
'Let me but kiss your eyes, my sweet, my sparrow.'
Even the man-sized ostrich some will know
20 As the sparrow-camel. Sparrowcide denotes
Destruction of sparrows. Preserve us from that crime.
Instead, let there be sparrowdom, the reign
Of sparrows, for sustaining your kin in name
At least suggests some worth in human habitations.

Characters

Sparrows wait on the garden seat for crumbs.
Their rather few toes rattle on the wood,
Not like the pigeons', red as blood, but pale
As mine. Are those two at the back called thumbs?

5 Their beaks proportionately seem as big
As toucans'. They sit legless on their tails,
But I can see their mandarins' nails stretched out;
Head-feathers untidy as a clever wig.

There are as many in the world as us:
10 Each one that riffles the air in landing here
Presents a character as clear as those
Of humankind I see wait for a bus.

An English Summer

Roberto Gerhard watched in his Cambridge garden
The changing evening light; and even called
His wife to observe some conjuror's effect.
Appreciative and patient immigrant!

5 The English summer passes for the English
In a succession of departing trains –
Attention fixed on the boredom of farewells
Or anguish of far-too-early, just-too-late.

What's rescuable from the wreckage of a year?
10 Earth-coloured infant blackbirds, wise in choice
Of colour; flower-beds in rainy dawns –
Yellows and mauves of Enna carried off
To the underworld; surviving fingers brown
From unremembered and unmanmade suns.

The Art of the Apple

The apple, stolid centre of assemblies
Of bottle, napkin, pipe, assumes in autumn
A more active role in art by casting
A pointilliste shadow for its tree, composed of
5   Blobs: green, blush-red, rotten-brown.

What forces you, apple-tree, to become a firework,
Throwing up coloured orbs that stay suspended –
The previous shower, not all extinguished,
Still on the ground; is your cylinder hollow,
10   In fact, though so gnarled and dense?

'Draw lines; whether from memory or after
Nature. Then you will be a good artist.' Thus
Ingres to Degas. The apple-tree is about
To reveal the rectilinear essence
15   Of its vague superstructure.

Confusing conspectus of periods and
Schools, how can we make up our minds about you?
Even plucking the compact heart from your depths
And biting its blend of flesh and sinew, sweet
20   And tart, leaves us uncertain.

Some monk in a past century grafted on,
Perhaps, to the original feeble crab
A vision of blossoming stigmata and
Miraculous food. One finds suspiciously
25   Romantic the concept now.

Creeper

A tendril's actually entered
The house, and faintly tinted it is
(A sinew or duct from deep inside
Some anatomy) compared to the
5   Shining magenta leaves on the wall.

These, hung in September stillness, have
Made the yellow brickwork reflect their
Flushing; and at death's approach, lesser
Leaves having fallen, show the tangled
10   Cordage with which they have been hoisted.

Probing filament, what do you seek
In our affairs? You have waited too
Long to arrive, in any event,
For your pallid reach must fail soon, not
15   Even leave a dry whisker, perhaps.

What a frail representative of
That serrate, cinquefoil splendour! Yet it
Can be seen that even the foetus
Shapes along your lank length have the same
20   Strange oneness of contour and number.

Undoubtedly in a season of
Dying the preparation, though much
Of it abortive, is for re-birth;
However perverse the confidence,
25   And grotesque the sacrifice of flesh.

Doesn't that reassure the body's
House, invaded by extending rods
Of foreign or unruly objects?
Or merely remind our furniture
30   Of the restless empire of nature?

83

Autobiography of a Lungworm

My normal dwelling is the lungs of swine,
   My normal shape a worm,
But other dwellings, other shapes, are mine
   Within my natural term.
5 Dimly I see my life, of all, the sign,
   Of better lives the germ.

The pig, though I am inoffensive, coughs,
   Finding me irritant:
My eggs go with the contents of the troughs
10   From mouth to excrement –
The pig thus thinks, perhaps, he forever doffs
   His niggling resident.

The eggs lie unconsidered in the dung
   Upon the farmyard floor,
15 Far from the scarlet and sustaining lung:
   But happily a poor
And humble denizen provides a rung
   To make ascension sure.

The earthworm eats the eggs; inside the warm
20   Cylinder larvae hatch:
For years, if necessary, in this form
   I wait the lucky match
That will return me to my cherished norm,
   My ugly pelt dispatch.

25 Strangely, it is the pig himself becomes
   The god inside the car:
His greed devours the earthworms; so the slums
   Of his intestines are
The setting for the act when clay succumbs
30   And force steers for its star.

The larvae burrow through the bowel wall
    And, having to the dregs
Drained ignominy, gain the lung's great hall.
    They change. Once more, like pegs,
35 Lungworms are anchored to the rise and fall
    – And start to lay their eggs.

What does this mean? The individual,
    Nature, mutation, strife?
I feel, though I am simple, still the whole
40   Is complex; and that life –
A huge, doomed throbbing – has a wiry soul
    That must escape the knife.

Notes

These notes were compiled in consultation with Roy Fuller to explain any references in the poems which are personal or otherwise arcane.

Diary Entries

These are not based on actual entries for a particular year, although they may all have been written within a single year.

ll.33–34. The actor who was listed in an old theatre programme in a minor part (Second Lord) has become famous.

ll.34–36. Roy Fuller's 'ancient verse' must be 'spurious', as it is, in the poet's view, so different from his later poetry.

l.38. The poet was eight when his father died. See 'Fathers', ll. 15–18 (p. 57).

Death of A Dictator

This poem operates at two levels. The dictator is any father whose children flee the home because of his oppressive strictness. Roy Fuller also had in mind the death of the Russian dictator, Joseph Stalin, who died on the 5th March, 1953. By the age of twenty Fuller was a Marxist (see pp. xiv-xvi), but, by the time of Stalin's death, his attitude to Communism was ambivalent. Here, he recognizes the atrocities committed by Stalin, the oppressive father, but the attraction of the communist promise of a more just society has not completely gone.

l.12. The deceits practised by Stalin merge with the ideals he represents: once again the poet's ambivalent attitude to the dictator.

At T.S. Eliot's Memorial Service

T.S. Eliot died on the 4th January, 1965, and a Memorial Service was held for him on the 4th February of that year. Jessie Weston's *From Ritual to Romance* (1920) was the source of much of the symbolism of one of Eliot's most famous poems, *The Waste Land*. The last phrase of the quotation suggests the oblique and mysterious nature of much poetry.

l.1. The service was held in Westminster Abbey.

ll.11–12. In *The Waste Land* Eliot made use of the myth of the Fisher King and the Legend of the Holy Grail, which he took from Jessie Weston's *From Ritual to Romance*. The Fisher King is a fertility cult figure, the wounded ruler whose land is laid waste and who struggles for salvation. The Grail is the cup said to have been used by Christ at the Last Supper. Joseph of Arimathea brought the cup to Glastonbury in the West of England and it was afterwards lost. It became part of the Arthurian Legend and the subject of many quests. The horrors in Chapel Perilous (l.12) are a test of the Knight's courage as he seeks the Grail. Roy Fuller's source is the following passage:

> (The hero) . . . meets with a strange and terrifying adventure in a mysterious Chapel, an adventure which, we are given to understand, is fraught with extreme peril to life. The details vary: sometimes there is a Dead Body laid on the altar . . .
>
> *(From Ritual to Romance*, p. 165.)

l.14. This line refers to Eliot's own death where the myth, so to speak catches up with him – he himself is on the altar.

l.19. head: i.e. the poet's.

ll.21–24. The poet went into Westminster Abbey from what, for him, is the familiar and well-loved entrance in Parliament Square (i.e. the Square), and came out into what he regards as ugly Victoria Street, full of business people (i.e. purgatory-crowded). They remind the poet of the encounter with Stetson in *The Waste Land* (ll.60–76) with its association with London Bridge and the City (i.e. the business) area. The message of *The Waste Land* which Roy Fuller creates in the last line is that nothing has changed: as before, the ruler is dying, the land dry, death triumphant.

Aberdeen Revisited

l.4. Roy Fuller was called up into the Navy in April 1941. He first went to *H.M.S. Ganges* (see 'Quatrains of an Elderly Man', ll.49–52, p. 18), and then to Chatham Barracks. From there, in June 1941, he went to Aberdeen on an electricity and wireless course. In November 1941, he left for Lee-on-the-Solent in Hampshire (see 'Waiting to be Drafted', p. 51). This, the poet's first visit to Aberdeen since that time, was occasioned by a Governors' Meeting of the B.B.C. (see p. xxiii).

l.6. square: a radar joke. One of the poet's jobs on his course was to build a wireless circuit which produces a sudden surge of energy which, equally suddenly, dies away. If displayed on a cathode ray oscilloscope, 'square' patterns would appear.

l.8. alma mater's: the course was held in Robert Gordon's College.

l.17. the Andrew: a naval name for the Navy.

Thirty Years On

l.8. Francis Scarfe, *Auden and After*, 1942. It contains brief mention of Roy Fuller.

l.9. Roy Fuller left England in March or April 1942 (see 'Waiting to be Drafted', p. 51) to be a radar mechanic with the Navy in Ceylon. As Japanese bombing had forced the Fleet back to Mombasa, he ended up in East Africa instead, returning to the United Kingdom for a commission in November, 1943.

l.14. Kenneth Allott was a poet of repute in the thirties who wrote little poetry after 1943. He spent most of his career as a don teaching English, and died in 1973.

l.32. Walt Whitman (1819–1892) wrote as a stretcher-bearer in the American Civil War: as the next line suggests, Whitman's night-passage would seem to be different from Roy Fuller's!

l.36. 'Too late. Too late.': from Kenneth Allott's 'Lament for A Cricket Eleven', in *Collected Poems* (1975).

l.37. The poet's father died on the 18th December, 1920: he was thirty-six.

In his Sixty-fifth Year

l.15. the Danish sage: Kierkegaard (1813–1855).

l.16. An ugly monarch may be so abashed by his physical appearance that he may not oppress his subjects . . .

l.21f. Georges Sorel (1847–1922), French social philosopher. The last sentence of his *Reflections on Violence* (1950) gives the flavour of Roy Fuller's point:

'It is to violence that Socialism owes those high ethical values by means of which it brings *salvation* to the modern world.' (p. 278).

l.26. The politicians (i.e. maniacs) who salute the march-past of missiles in the October parade in Red Square, Moscow.

l.43. Desert Island Discs is a long-running radio programme (still on Radio 4) where a visiting celebrity is invited by Roy Plomley to select eight records he would take to a desert island.

l.48. Johnny Mercer (1909–1976), singer and composer of popular lyrics and music.

l.53. gold: i.e. very hot.

l.70. Jerome David Kern (188–1945). His song, 'They Didn't Believe Me' in *The Girl from Utah* (first performed in 1913) has been described as setting a basic pattern for all modern show songs (Gerald Bordman, *Jerome Kern*, 1980).

l.71. Enrique Granados (l.42) and his wife were returning home on the liner *Sussex* from New York where they had just seen the première of his opera, *Goyescas*, when the liner was sunk by a German submarine.

l.74. From the Johnny Mercer song, 'Early Autumn'.

On his Sixty-fifth Birthday

This poem is modelled on Matthew Arnold's pindaric odes, such as *Rugby Chapel*.

l.1. A Mini-Town Hall performs some of the functions of a Town Hall: The one referred to here is in Greenwich.

l.11. Previously printed as:

> Befitting their unamorous age.

ll.12–13. Greenwich Mini-Town Hall is set in Kidbrooke Park Road off the Dover road (A2).

ll.38–43. These lines refer to four of Matthew Arnold's pindaric odes: *Rugby Chapel, The Youth of Nature, Heine's Grave* (Heine is the 'Kraut' of l.41), and *Haworth Churchyard*.

ll.44–46. Previously printed as:

> For arraigning England he forgave
> Heine-since 'we echo her foes' . . .

l.44. arraigning:

> I chide with three not, that thy sharp
> Upbraidings often assailed
> England, my country . . .
>
> > *Heine's Grave*, ll.70–72.

l.46. 'Echo the blame of her foe'. *Ibid.*, l.75.

l.49. 'Glory, and genius, and joy'. *Ibid.*, l.84.

l.72. Previously printed as:

> 'Him where daffodils all look south.'

ll.96–97.

> Charm is the glory which makes
> Song of the poets divine,
> Love is the fountain of charm.

Heine's Grave, ll.103–105.

ll. 108 and 113. references to the River Styx, boundary of the Greek underworld.

Quatrains of an Elderly Man

l.8. Characters in Dickens' *Great Expectations*.

ll.33–34. Roy Fuller based these lines on a Deutsche Grammophon sleeve-note where it says that 'Brahms described as cradle songs of his sorrow' Op. 117, 118 and 119 ('Wiegenlieder seines Schmerzes bezeichnete').

ll.39–40. A reference to John Donne's comparison of loved ones to a pair of compasses in 'A Valediction: Forbidding Mourning', ll.25–36.

l.49f. See note to 'Aberdeen Revisited', l.4.

To an Unknown Reader

ll.47–48. Yankee: Ralph Waldo Emerson. The line is taken from his 'Ode: inscribed to W.H. Channing'.

Jag and Hangover

'Jag' is slang for 'spree' or 'night-out'.

ll.21–22. A reference to *Rumpelstiltskin*, a fairy story of the Brothers Grimm. The Miller's daughter, later a princess, being set the task of turning straw into gold, did not know how to do it, but was helped by the dwarf, Rumpelstiltskin.

l.34. Tribunes: politicians.

Dialogue of the Poet and his Talent

ll.14–15. 'Faced with historical forces of such a kind, the contemporary individual feels utterly helpless; as a rule he falls into the bondage either of the aggressor or of the defender. Few are the contemporaries who can attain an Archimedean point outside events, and are able to "overcome in the spirit".' Jakob Burckhardt, *Reflections on History* (1943), p. 19.

Dead Poet

The poet referred to is C. Day Lewis, 1904–1972, associated with Auden and the 'new poetry' movement of the Thirties, Poet Laureate 1968–1972.

l.1. i.e. walking across Blackheath.

Poet and Reader

l.1. This is the last poem in *Counterparts* (1954), and the first stanza poses a hypothetical reader's possible reaction to the volume.

The Poet: His Public

l.2. Roy Fuller's first volume of poetry for children, (1972).

Chekhov

The poet is thinking in particular of the end of *The Cherry Orchard*.

Rhetoric of a Journey

This poem, as so many of Roy Fuller's, works at two levels. It records the poet's return to London after a visit to his ailing mother in the north. The train leaves the Pennine valleys between Lancashire and Yorkshire (the northern valleys, l.1), travelling down through the Midlands (the central plain, l.75). The poem also records the passage of years from youth to middle age.

l.37. The poet had in mind the sons of eminent Victorians shipped off to Australia.

l.88. a rattle of tin: the poet had in mind a tray of tea.

Florestan to Leonora

See pp. xvii–xviii.

This poem is a dramatic monologue where the Florestan of Beethoven's opera, *Fidelio*, speaks to his wife, Leonora.

l.1. cage: see pp. xvii–xviii.

l.2. The minister, Don Fernando, had come to the prison to rescue Florestan.

l.5. jackboots: Leonora, disguised as a man, is presented in jackboots. Although the Stuttgart performance created an atmosphere suggestive of Nazism, 'jackboots' is not intended by the poet to refer to the fascists. Leonora's life loses its heroic aspects and returns to normality.

l.7. impossible task: Florestan argues that his love would have allowed him to attempt what Leonora had achieved (l.8), but that it is impossible for him simply to accept what she has done forhim, impossible for his love to accept 'the gift it did not ask'. He has become used to imprisonment: freedom, particularly when given in this way, is difficult.

l.10. trumpet: the Minister's arrival had been announced by a trumpet call.

The Ides of March

See p. xvii.

A dramatic monologue spoken by the Brutus of Shakespeare's *Julius Caesar* at the start of Act 2, Scene I, as it were. The scene is set in Brutus' orchard.

l.1. In *Julius Caesar*, Act I ends with thunder and lightning.

l.29. An oblique reference to the legend that Brutus was Caesar's natural son. See p. xvii.

Expostulation and Inadequate Reply

ll.9–10. Roy Fuller has in mind the immediate post-Second World War generation of poets of the late Forties.

Dedicatory Epistle with a Book of 1949

Epitaphs and Occasions (1949).

l.38. coward's cold: Behind this and 1.40 is the idea Fuller found in the work of the German psychologist, Georg Groddeck, that all illness is pscyhological.

l.74. A cricketing line. Somerset had a reputation for batsmen who hit out, Lancashire for stonewallers.

l.80. A reference to Mozart's *Don Giovanni*.

l.107. Sassoon's early poetry was 'poetic' in a heightened sense ('Georgian style'). He became dissatisfied with this – 'napoo' is a First World War Expression meaning 'no use' – and his verse became more realistic.

Translation

The title does not mean that the poem is translated: it indicates that it is a statement about another age. The 'I' is Cinna, the poet in Shakespeare's *Julius Caesar*.

l.1. Picra: a place-name selected by the poet 'almost at random' from Lemprière's *Classical Dictionary*.

To George Woodcock, in his and the Author's Sixty-fifth Year
What Marxian spectre lays its beard on the evening? is l.13 of George
Woodcock's poem, 'Wartime Evening in Cambridge', put here by Roy
Fuller to amuse his friend.
ll.1–3. Antonio Gramsci was an Italian communist arrested by the fas-
cists in 1926 and who died in prison in 1937. His *Lettere dal carcere*
(Letters from Prison) were first published in 1946.
ll.15–19. 'Avoid shabby attire, long hair, an unkempt beard, an out-
spoken dislike of silverware, sleeping on the ground and all other mis-
guided means to self-advertisement.' Letter 5 in Seneca: *Letters from a
Stoic* (Penguin Books 1969).
l.29. Bruch's schmalz. Listening to Max Bruch's *First Violin Concerto* on
tape reminds Roy Fuller of those times when he used to listen to the same
piece played by two friends, a pianist and a fiddler. See *Souvenirs*, pp.
97–98.
ll.37–40. In a letter to Tatiana (Tania Schucht) from Ustica, dated the 9th
December, 1926.
ll. 51–57. See Gramsci's letter to Tania from Milan, dated the 21st
November, 1927.

First Air-Raids
The impulse behind this poem is the poet's being separated from his wife
at the beginning of the Second World War.
l.14. curtain. A reference to Hamlet's killing of Polonius through the
arras, and the curtain as a symbol of domestic defences during the war.

Battersea: After Dunkirk, June 3 1940
ll.12–14. The slaves of Egyptian times were capable of building huge
pyramids, but lacked power. The poet sees the modern working-class in a
parallel position. In 1940, he sees the world in such a state that he feels a
new society must come out of the old.

The Phoney War
l.1. Belphégor,(trans. by S.J.I. Lawson, Payson and Clarke Ltd., New
York, 1929.) *ll.20–21.* are taken from the Foreword to *Belphégor*:

On the contrary, it would seem that
war intensifies the craving for emotion.

93

l.11. The minor poets of the Thirties who wrote 'Doom' and lived on to see it.

Waiting to Be Drafted
Written in 1942 in a naval establishment near Lee-on-the-Solent. See note to 'Aberdeen Revisited', l.4, and to 'Thirty Years On', l.9.
l.8. The mauve island: the Isle of Wight in the evening light.

Y.M.C.A. Writing Room
l.1. lying: as a map the world looks calm and unmoving but in reality it is a theatre of war. The poet is also thinking of the distortions involved in Mercator's Projection.
l.4. blues and reds: see pp. xvi–xvii.
l.5. friends: those who had come to Lee-on-the-Solent (from Aberdeen) to complete the secret part of the radar course. Cf. 'Waiting to be Drafted'.

During a Bombardment by V-Weapons
ll.9–12. To the poet war is a temporary fury. The thought that illness or death will take away his wife worries him more.

Memories of War
It is the mid-Seventies: the poet is in Lewisham Hospital.
l.15. proximately: cf. the use of 'ope' in 'On his Sixty-fifth Birthday', l. 34.

Confrontation off Korea, 1968
On the 23rd January, 1968, North Korea seized the U.S. naval intelligence ship, *Pueblo*, causing a major international incident. The nuclear-powered aircraft carrier *Enterprise* and other American warships were ordered into the area of Wonsan, and President Johnson called up reserves and summoned an emergency meeting of the U.N. Security Council.

Fathers
l.2. The poet was eight.

The Card-Table
l.36. From Franz Lehar's *The Merry Widow*.

Family Matters

l.4. a small hotel: 'The Anchorage' on the Fylde Coast. Cf. *Souvenirs*, p. 78.

l.15. In 1919 (possibly 1918), the Fullers moved into Waterhead on the outskirts of Oldham, but just within the Yorkshire side of the border. Cf. *Souvenirs*, p 24.

l.25. His mother and maternal grandmother.

ll.25–26. His maternal grandfather was a local government councillor.

The Family Cat

l.1. This cat: Figaro.

l.2. 2nd September, 1945.

Nino, The Wonder Dog

An actual variety turn which the poet had seen at Lewisham Hippodrome.

Road Safety

1.6. three-badge stoker: an old-timer. In the Navy, the three stripes signify long service.

On the Mountain

See pp. xviii–xix.

Here the poet sees, through Constantine the Great, Emperor of Rome 306–337, parallels between his own times and those of Constantine's Rome. His source for the Roman element is Moses Hadas' translation of Jacob Burckhardt's *The Age of Constantine the Great* (1949). He sees four main parallels: bad art, eccentric behaviour, price fixing, and concern over who will succeed.

l.74. famous peak: some such mountain as Mont Blanc, whose outline is well-known.

ll.75–78. The climber cannot see the curve of history because he is concerned with the day-to-day business of living.

Oxford Album

Roy Fuller was Oxford Professor of Poetry from 1968 to 1973.

l.1. Magdalen College.

l.7. dwarfs: the works of J.R.R. Tolkien such as *The Lord of the Rings*.

l.7. little girls: Lewis Carroll's *Alice in Wonderland*.

l.12. emperors: Fuller intends a reference to the sculpted heads outside the Sheldonian Theatre.
l.13. yellows: the colour of the dominant Oxford building material.
l.14. fenestrated twirls: the pillars around the College windows.
l.15. the strangled artery: the High Street, full of Colleges and traffic.

Books and Discs
ll.16–17. From Purcell's *The Indian Queen*.

The Night Sky in August 1980
Based on 'The night sky in August' in *The Times*, 31st July, 1980, p. 16. It is not just the quoted lines which are from the report:

> Meteor watching is not a matter of a few minutes, so make yourself comfortable in a deck chair facing north-east.

Abbas
ll.17–18. Haydn is sometimes known as 'Papa Haydn', but in this case, argues the poet, it cannot be appropriate, as Haydn was thirty-nine at the time of composing.
l.47. perennial Turk: Karlheinz Stockhausen, born 1928.

Pictures of Winter
l.1. See p. xviii.
ll.3. the gallery's: Tate gallery
l.28. queen's: Persephone.

Hedge-sparrows and House-sparrows
This poem is based around certain entries under 'hedge-sparrow' in the Oxford *New English Dictionary*.
ll.4–5. pyramids: the bills of house-sparrows are better adapted for eating seeds than those of hedge-sparrows.
l.18. The one entry under 'Sparrow 1(b) Used as a term of endearment' in the *N.E.D.* is from the Rev. Alexander Dyce's 1842 edition of the early seventeenth century comedy, *Timon*:

> Lett me but kisse thyne eyes, my sweete delight
> My sparrow ... my duck, my cony.

l.20. sparrow-camel. Under 4(b) as an obsolete term.

l.1. Roberto Gerhard, a Spanish composer, lived in exile in Cambridge from 1938 until his death.

Biographical Note

1912	Roy Broadbent Fuller, born the 11th February, in Failsworth, Lancashire.
1923–28	Educated at Blackpool High School.
1933	Qualified as a solicitor.
1936	Married Kathleen Smith.
1937	John Fuller, his only child, born in Ashford, Kent.
1938–58	Assistant Solicitor, Woolwich Equitable Building Society.
1939	*Poems.*
1941–46	Served in the Royal Navy.
1942–43	Radar mechanic in East Africa.
1942	*The Middle of a War.*
1944–46	Lieutenant in the Royal Naval Volunteer Reserve at the Admiralty, London.
1944	*A Lost Season.*
1946	*Savage Gold.*
1948	*With my Little Eye.*
1949	*Epitaphs and Occasions.*
1953	*The Second Curtain.*
1954	*Fantasy and Fugue.*
1954	*Counterparts.*
1956	*Image of a Society.*
1957	*Brutus's Orchard.*
1958–69	Solicitor, Woolwich Equitable Building Society.
1958–69	Chairman, Legal Advisory Panel of the Building Societies' Association.
1958	Fellow, Royal Society of Literature.
1959	*The Ruined Boys.*
1960–68	Chairman, Poetry Book Society.
1961	*The Father's Comedy.*
1962	*Collected Poems, 1936–1961*

1963	*The Perfect Fool.*
1965	*My Child, my Sister.*
1965	*Buff.*
1966	*Catspaw.*
1968–73	Professor of Poetry, Oxford University.
1968	*New Poems.*
1969	Director, Woolwich Equitable Building Society.
1969	A Vice-President, Building Societies' Association.
1969	*Off Course.*
1970	C.B.E. (Commander, Order of the British Empire).
1970	*The Carnal Island.*
1971	*Owls and Artificers: Oxford Lectures on Poetry.*
1972	*Seen Grandpa Lately?*
1972–79	A Governor of the B.B.C.
1973	*Tiny Tears.*
1973	*Professors and Gods: Last Oxford Lectures on Poetry.*
1974	*An Old War.*
1975	*From the Joke Shop.*
1975	*The Joke Shop Annexe.*
1976	*An Ill-governed Coast.*
1976–77	Chairman, Literature Panel of the Arts Council.
1977	*Poor Roy.*
1979	*The Other Planet.*
1980	*The Reign of Sparrows.*
1980	*Souvenirs.*
1981	*More about Tompkins.*